Inspiring, informative books for thoughtful readers wanting to make changes and realise their potential.

Other titles in the series include:

Living the Life You Want
Your personal key to true abundance and richness of everyday experience

Thinking Straight
A systematic guide to managerial problem-solving and decision-making that works

When What You've Got Is Not What You Want
Use NLP to create the life you want and live it to the full

Choosing a Better Life
An inspiring step-by-step guide to building the future you want

Building Your Life Skills
Who are you, where are you, and where do you want to go: a personal action plan

Please send for a free copy of the catalogue for full details
(see back cover for address).

Achieve Twice as Much in Half the Time

Achieve Twice as Much in Half the Time

Practical new ways to maximise your time and transform your life

Dr Harry Alder

PATHWAYS

First published in 2001 by
How To Books Ltd, 3 Newtec Place,
Magdalen Road, Oxford OX4 1RE, United Kingdom
Tel: 01865 793806 Fax: 01865 248780

British Library Cataloguing in Publication Data
A catalogue record for this book is available from
the British Library

Edited by Diana Brueton / Cover image PhotoDisc
Cover design by Shireen Nathoo Design

Produced for How To Books by Deer Park Productions
Typeset by PDQ Typesetting, Newcastle-under-Lyme
Printed and bound in Great Britain by The Baskerville Press Ltd.

Note: The material contained in this book is set out in good
faith for general guidance and no liability can be accepted for
loss or expenses incurred as a result of relying in particular
circumstances on statements made in the book. The laws and
regulations are complex and liable to change, and readers
should check the current position with the relevant
authorities before making personal arrangements.

Pathways is an imprint of
How To Books

Contents

List of Illustrations

Preface

We have all experienced times of personal excellence, or 'flow', when we achieved many times our normal output, and took any barriers in our stride. On such occasions it is not unusual to accomplish twice as much in half the time. Sadly, these times – for most of us – are all too rare. And we can't produce them 'on tap'. Imagine being able to call upon these productive powers, consciously and consistently. Time management problems, as such, would be over. That's what this book is about.

The principles and techniques you will learn are based upon extensive research among top business achievers, plus recent research into the working of the human mind. That makes it a very different sort of time management book. It is concerned with the way successful people think, the way they get better than average results from their standard brain. It uncovers aspects of top leaders and prodigious achievers that don't get into time management books. This especially includes the powerful effect of unconscious thinking, and the kind of thinking associated with the right side of the brain, and with imagination and creativity.

Understanding the way we think can bring about important changes in every aspect of our behaviour, including how we use our time and what we achieve. Learning to make better use of this latent, creative side of our thinking can open up opportunities for dramatic improvement in individual performance.

The right side of the brain has had a bad press. It is like the dark side of the moon that was once mystical and unknown. It has no place for the language and logical patterns that are the familiar currency of the dominant left brain.

Many time management books ignore the thought processes that go on below the surface. But what goes on in our subconscious mind inevitably results in real behaviour (or lack of behaviour), and, for better or worse, real happenings – outcomes – in our lives.

These thought processes include our feelings, attitudes and beliefs. We are often aware of these to some degree, yet cannot really understand them, let alone fully control them. This book tackles these topics head-on in a practical way. It shows you how, for instance, to identify the self-beliefs that affect your behaviour and performance, and then to make any necessary changes.

Other thought processes, such as intuition, 'gut feelings', 'insights', so-called 'eurekas', or 'sleeping on the problem', can also have a major effect on everything we do. More often than not, however, we tend to suppress and under-utilise these potential aids to creative thinking and problem-solving.

The main purpose of this book is to enable you to harness the full power of your whole brain – including the under-utilised right side, which in many people seems to have atrophied. With such holistic thinking you can start to achieve what hitherto might have seemed impossible.

Time, we shall see, is not usually the real problem. Indeed, time can become a friend as you convert it, moment by moment, into bigger and better outcomes, by achieving more within it. Achieving what you want in an effective, creative, imaginative way is at the heart of the matter.

Some of the chapter headings will look familiar. In fact there is a remarkable uniformity of topics in books about time management. Unfortunately, the standard prescriptions do not seem to bring about long-term change, even when a lot of effort is applied. However, I address each familiar topic from a lateral, or 'right-brain' angle, sometimes turning the received wisdom on its head.

Sensory visualisation of an important goal, for example, is a very different sort of planning technique to writing down your goals, or, indeed, 'affirming' them each morning in front of the mirror. As we shall see, it can be infinitively more effective, and also more pleasurable, than traditional goal-achieving processes. Other topics I cover, such as 'downtime', associated with preoccupation or daydreaming, and incubation, or sleeping on a problem, might not even get a mention in a standard time management book, yet are indispensable aspects of human achievement.

Self-belief is another crucial aspect of managing your time. This alone may well represent the difference between mediocrity and excellence, between those for whom time is a master and those for whom it is a friend and ally. Fortunately, self-belief is neither genetic nor immutable. It's something you can develop as you grow in self-knowledge and the sorts of mental skills described in this book.

The principle is that we use it or lose it. Nor surprisingly, our research found consistent evidence of such thinking phenomena in leaders and the most successful time managers. If we wish to have more control over our own destiny, we need to have more control over how we think, and in particular over our unconscious right brain. This book will give you the understanding you need, providing the necessary practical techniques to achieve this control and the personal excellence that will follow.

Dr Harry Alder

CHAPTER 1

The Secret of Top Achievers

A level of productivity some three or four times the norm. Priceless ideas that save both effort and time. The euphoria of being in control – being effective. It's a great feeling when you are operating at peak performance and it produces extraordinary results. But how do you achieve it *when you need to*?

Think about that sinking feeling that comes over you when you know you'll just never make it. Imagine the not uncommon scenario: in a few days you will leave the office for a well-earned holiday, but first you have a mountain of work to clear. And you know what that can mean: frantically chasing around but getting nowhere, mental blocks just when you need a clear head, seeming to actually go backwards the more effort you put in. And, just to turn the screw, you know only too well how a holiday can be ruined by the mental baggage and guilt of unfinished work at the office.

But something happens. Something inside you (as the outside world seems the same). By Friday finishing time you are off on holiday, fairly skipping out of the place, having achieved, even though you say it yourself, miracles. It's an extraordinary achievement against all the odds and contrary to all the rules of time management.

You wish you could do it all the time, or at least a bit more frequently. Yet it's quite a common phenomenon. For instance, something similar happens when you are given a task with a deadline that is completely non-negotiable, and which maybe could affect your job and career. You *can't imagine* what would happen if you didn't achieve it, so you've got to *imagine achieving it* – or you'll give up before you start. Whatever the logic, and whatever your best track record dictates, you believe (because you daren't not believe) it will and therefore can happen. So 'miracles' of time management take place.

> The deadline – or the perceived deadline – seems to make all the difference.

There is something that conceives the motivation, ingenuity, single-mindedness and whatever else produces the extraordinary results. That 'something', once identified and harnessed, could revolutionise your life.

Using your brain in a different way

In these deadline situations you *simply use your brain in a different way.* Everything you do on these occasions is legitimate and makes management sense. There is no mystique or magic. Any corners you cut, work you delegate, or timesaving techniques you adopt, you could have been doing all the time. The real mystery is that you don't work in that way all the time, even though the pressure is there, and the workload, and time is always at a premium. You have the experience and skills, which are exactly what you drew upon to accomplish what you did before your holiday. But feelings, attitudes, motivation – whatever – play a big part. Technical skills and even long experience take on secondary status. Somehow thoughts take over.

A *way of thinking*, including attitudes and beliefs, makes the crucial difference. Thoughts take the form of beliefs – beliefs about what you are capable of. Thoughts motivate – or demotivate – you. Thoughts determine:

◆ what you really want to accomplish
◆ your priorities in life
◆ what's important.

Such thoughts are the secret of how top achievers manage their time. Operating and controlling these ordinary thinking processes – with or without a holiday coming up on Friday – are the special skills you will learn in this book.

In modern life and business a volatile, changing environment is the rule rather than the exception. So if you aspire to excellence in a world as competitive as it is staggeringly complex, sequential, logical thinking *alone* (the legacy of decades of 'scientific management') is not enough. Computers do it quite well anyway. It has certainly not provided answers to the age-old time management problem. Instead, we need to think creatively, and that involves breaking up old patterns of thought and being ready to use new ones. We have to be ready to do this whenever the environment changes, which is most mornings.

At the mercy of how you feel

One day you might feel good, although there is no particular reason for it, and you produce prodigious outputs of work. Another day you feel 'a bit under' and all the willpower you can muster has no effect. Nor does 'trying harder' (the education system's panacea for struggling scholars). Self-consciously trying harder may even make matters worse. You get to the end of the day wondering if you have achieved anything at all.

Your skills and experience are not in question – or at least they are clearly not the real problem, and you can do something about them anyway. Instead, you seem to be at the mercy of how you feel, or whatever is going on in your mind below the surface. Here's the stark fact: however much we may try to rationalise and psych ourselves up, it seems there are great chunks of our behaviour that are firmly outside our control.

> The solution to the 'time' problem – and much else besides – lies in harnessing mental powers to achieve conscious, positive goals, by intelligent processes rather than by accident or default.

Short-term 'drivers', or 'motivators', like a five o'clock deadline, an imminent holiday, or a career-significant demand from the boss, may well play their part. But self-confidence and belief – the way we think – are at the centre of time and self-management. These can be developed and cultivated, but they call for a very different approach. Doubling your usefulness to the world may require no less than a personal transformation, and a radically different way of seeing things. You need to be prepared to take such a new perspective if you are to achieve twice as much in half the time – in fact, if you are to bring about any significant change for the better.

The mark of a successful person

Managing personal time is one of the biggest single issues facing people today. The massive delayering that has taken place in most organisations has increased personal responsibility and reduced the scope for delegation, a prime time management until a few years ago. Much more is now demanded of staff and managers who thought they had already reached the limit of what they could achieve in the time available. Managing time is every bit as important to busy housewives, schoolchildren and college students, self-employed people, and those handling a normal range of social commitments. Being able to *use time to the full* is what really marks out a successful person.

The Archbishop of Canterbury, Dr George Carey, left school at 15 without formal qualifications. Yet he later clocked up three GCE A levels and six O levels in just one year. My research among business leaders uncovered similar cases of achievement. Such 'impossible' levels of attainment are directly linked to time management skills, and seem to be a feature of top leadership roles. Yet leaders repeatedly deny that they were born with special gifts. However, whatever brings about such prodigious time management feats in those we see as successful, their 'outputs' exceed those of other industrious and talented colleagues by enormous margins. This wide gap resembles that which exists between the 'up times' and 'down times' in our own individual experience. Put another way, successful people are simply more *consistent* in pulling off the highly productive 'flow' experience.

A different approach

The aim of this book is to help you release extra time so that you can do more of what you like doing best. This might mean greater output in your main paid job, doing the many things that you never get round to doing. Or it may mean extra time channelled into a favourite hobby or pastime. Or simply more leisure time with your family or to spend alone. Such freedom in choosing how to spend your time becomes less common and more valuable as life gets more hectic. But it is possible to regain control, and start living the life you want to live. You can't achieve it without managing yourself and your time, and this book will show you how.

> This special approach is concerned with how we think, and in particular with how the intuitive, creative powers of the mind can be stimulated and harnessed.

In some cases this means standing a lot of accepted time management wisdom on its head. In other cases I simply give a different perspective, which may work better for you than techniques you have tried in the past.

Readers who do not like to follow rigid rules but who enjoy exercising their own individual creativity, in particular, will find plenty of ways to build on this preference. Readers who do want to follow a neat formula will not find one. Personal transformation doesn't come neatly packaged with things to do and rules to follow. That's why it eludes thousands of conscientious 'tryers'. It involves knowing and being, and may mean profound changes in your life. However, if you are willing to undergo that sort of a transformation I can guarantee that personal productivity will follow.

A right-brain approach

The way we process thought using the right-side brain can be described as holistic. It is not conscious thinking – rational, logical and sequential. That happens on the left side, which deals in symbols such as language and numbers. Nor is this the way we usually 'think about thinking'. We usually associate thinking with *conscious* thought, which again happens largely in the left brain. Amazingly, the left and right sides of the upper brain operate in completely different ways. Figure 1 shows how they 'specialise' in doing certain things.

Flow thinking

Right-brain thinking does not involve conscious effort or 'trying'. On the contrary, the sort of behaviour and productivity we are concerned with seems to get worse the harder you try. We are at our most productive when in a state of what has been termed 'flow'. This applies in all sorts of situations – from

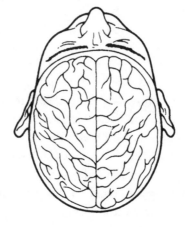

Left brain   Right brain

MODES OF THINKING

Left brain	Right brain
Deals with verbal ideas and uses words to describe things	Aware of things but does not connect them with words – uses gestures or pictures in description
Analyses: breaks things down into their constituent parts	Synthesises: puts parts together to form a whole
Uses symbols to represent things	Sees things as they are
Abstracts relevant pieces of information from the whole	Makes analogies and sees likenesses
Good sense of time	Poor sense of time
Relies on facts and reasoning	Relies on intuition and instinct
Good sense of numbers	Poor sense of numbers
Poor sense of spatial relationships	Good senses of spatial relationships
Logical	Intuitive
Thinks linearly – one idea follows another	Thinks holistically – sees patterns linking ideas as a whole

Fig. 1. Right-brain/left-brain modes of thinking.

sport to handling a complex work project, or just clearing out the attic.

However, there is a paradox that applies to this state of peak performance, and to right-brain thinking generally, which we all experience from time to time. For all the copious amounts of work we get through in no time at all, we don't seem to feel any strain or pain. It comes easy. And, just as important for present purposes, *time is not a problem*. It is not even a major factor.

In these situations it seems we *create* rather than use up energy. We certainly do not follow rigorous time management rules at such times, or indeed any other rules. What we do best, it seems, we do naturally and with enjoyment. Even the most difficult and distasteful jobs become enjoyable when we get the better of them through state of mind. Belief, or whatever – as we shall see – makes the difference. We also do them in a fraction of the time it usually takes.

Output thinking

The approach you will learn is not about five or ten per cent improvements here and there – marginal or incremental improvements. I do not dispute that such improvements are quite feasible using conventional time management techniques. However, these are not in the same league as the extra output we have all personally experienced from time to time – even if only rarely or unpredictably. Marginal improvements of that sort are not the subject of this book. I am only concerned with *substantial* improvement, with *doubling or more average* personal output.

Some people talk of increasing their output when they 'feel' right, believe they can achieve a tight deadline, or are fully committed to an outcome. Some talk of producing at three or four times their normal level. Others again talk of achieving, in a certain state and under certain conditions, goals that are 'beyond themselves', that they would not have accomplished 'in a hundred years'. Such events are usually accompanied by *ideas* ('brainwaves', 'inspiration', 'insights') that save time and energy, and sometimes tackle a problem in a novel, surprising way.

These are the sorts of phenomena we need to harness for

regular use. For all practical purposes your mind – which is where the clever stuff happens – has no limits.

> With the right know-how, you need settle for no less than the best you are capable of.

Radical solutions

This approach does not fit neatly with logic, systems or structures. You can't treble your output by tuning up a system. Even changing the entire 'system' will typically just produce marginal gains. The very best solutions to problems are creative, surprising and radical. Or at least they appear so when someone first thinks of them. They usually occur automatically when we are in a *mental state* of 'flow' or super-productivity. As such, these special times cannot even be understood or communicated, let alone converted into a 'system'. If you can systematise a brainwave, fine. If you can turn it into a routine task or behaviour, better still. But don't pretend it is still a brainwave. Yesterday's brainwave will be of little use as you face today's new problems and new, impossible deadlines.

The best 'systems' are:

◆ internal mental strategies
◆ habits that repeatedly help you to achieve what you want to.

A system for being optimistic, positive, or motivated is infinitely more valuable than one for retrieving files more quickly. You will learn how to elicit these success strategies, from yourself and others, as blueprints for consistent achievement.

You are responsible

Holistic thinking concerns *all* of you. *You* are central, not a technique or system, or even a mind-blowing principle or model, which is supposed to work for everyone. Most time management training follows the clichéd 'self-management not time management' route. The approach you will take concerns every nuance of your personal values, beliefs, attitudes and feelings. *Your perception*, for example, of a deadline, or a reward, or of what is urgent or important, is subjective and unique. That means you are at the heart of how you use your time and what you achieve with your life.

This places a lot of responsibility on you as an individual, whatever the outside circumstances. But you can treat this positively. The one vestige of control we seem to have in a fairly uncontrollable world is over what and how we *think*. By better understanding this resource, you will discover some very useful shortcuts to achievement, whatever time pressure you face.

Don't try too hard

Achievement doesn't depend upon effort. Maybe it should, but that doesn't concern us here. Effort is sometimes a factor, but even when it is it's the *direction* in which we apply it that brings about success – and effort can't help in that sort of decision. Many of the insights upon which successful behaviour and the 'flow' experience we described earlier are based come as 'gifts'. We don't *earn* them. They seem almost to come from outside of you ('it just came to me in a flash').

This something for nothing concept goes against the grain of the work ethic. It sits uneasily with the analytical, activity-based, conspicuously busy and sometimes macho mode of the modern executive. But think back to the times you have been most productive. Recall times you have been riding on a 'can-do' high and have surprised yourself by your sheer inventiveness and ingenuity. Whatever 'effort' you needed *did not seem like effort*. And that is the important difference when you use your brain in the right way.

The unpredictability of these times of special creativity renders them too mystical and intangible for the analytically trained person, who prefers the sweat and effort of marginal gains. But that isn't a sensible approach. We now know how important these factors are in all sorts of human achievement. It makes sense to get to know what is happening – especially what happens inside you – and to use *the system* for more conscious, positive outcomes.

Even a cursory study of top performers in all walks of life

will confirm that 'trying harder' is not the secret of their excellence. Quite the contrary. Sometimes they make it all easy and enjoyable.

> Conscious effort, for most people, might be better invested in *unlearning* redundant thinking habits and deliberately seeing things from new perspectives.

In the heat of day-to-day deadlines we need to learn to trust our virtually unlimited mind-power.

There are important implications in this different approach to time management. Any claim has to feel right, to have a ring of truth, if it is to be given a fair trial in practice. In the next chapter, therefore, I compare 'received wisdom' and conventional time management training topics with this not-so-common, holistic way of 'output' thinking.

Try it now

Spend about six minutes writing down your strong points and your weak points in terms of time management. Be as frank as possible. Let the following questions trigger your mind. This will be a very small investment of your time, but could be the basis for big changes.

1. Do you spend your time in the way you want?
2. Do you regularly work long hours?
3. Do you bring work home more than one night a week?
4. Do you regularly feel stress at work, even when there isn't a serious problem or crisis?
5. Do you feel guilty because you don't do as much work as you think you should, or that your boss thinks you should?
6. Do you set up short- and long-term objectives?
7. Do you like your work?
8. Does your work bring you satisfaction?
9. Do you take the time to stay physically in shape?
10. Can you clear your desk of papers in less than a minute – putting them where they should go, of course?
11. Are there papers on your desk that aren't important, which have been there for some time?
12. Do you often get letters or memos starting with 'In view of the fact that we have not received your response to our communication dated . . .', or similar words?

13. Are you often interrupted in the middle of important jobs?
14. Do you allow your colleagues to come into your office at any time of day?
15. Do you often take longer-than-necessary lunch breaks?
16. Do you eat in the office?
17. Have you forgotten any important appointments, or the dates of meetings, in the last month?
18. Do you often put off important jobs to the very last minute then work like mad to get them done?
19. Is it easy for you to make excuses for putting off doing things you dislike?
20. Do you have enough time to get away for long weekends, and to take the holidays you feel you need?
21. Do you have enough time for your favourite pastimes?
22. Do you have enough free time?
23. Do you take pleasure in the 'here and now'?
24. Do you always feel you should be doing something to keep busy?
25. Do you feel guilty when you rest for a long time?
26. Do you try to read carefully everything that appears on your desk?
27. Are there journals and other professional reading that you never get round to?
28. Do you have to finish or check work you ask your staff to do?
29. Do you deal with important company objectives, or with minor problems?
30. Do you have time to think about your methods and make improvements?
31. Do you feel in command of the situation, or that it is in command of you?

Managing time
means
managing your
brain, which
controls all your
behaviour.

CHAPTER 2

A Better Way to Manage Time

M any organisations have made great advances in customer focus and product quality. But something has gone wrong at a more fundamental level – *managing time*. Managers, for instance, are no more competent at time management now than when they first stepped onto the ladder of executive responsibility. Indeed, with all their training, management techniques and experience, some have gone backwards. Many say they are more swamped by work than ever. When workload increases along with staff cutbacks there is often bitterness, which makes the problems seem even worse.

This chapter introduces a more effective approach to managing your time. This approach takes account of how we actually think and habitually behave and can lead to radical improvements in output. The right-brain thinking described in the previous chapter is what we shall concentrate on, and later in this chapter you can do a simple exercise to check whether you have a particular preference for left- or right-brain thinking.

To judge by the proliferation of training courses, time management, perhaps along with 'finance for non-financial managers', must be one of the most 'trainable' of all management subjects. It is particularly alarming, therefore, that many of the training courses and books that are available do not fulfil what they promise. This is what I hear repeatedly from hundreds of managers around the world attending my seminars, and those of colleagues. Any improvement lasts perhaps a couple of weeks, and then old habits prevail over fancy new techniques. The systems and gadgets that accompanied the training are shelved, along with sincere resolutions – and not a little self-worth.

> When your self-image gets hit, your doubts are simply reconfirmed: 'I'm just hopeless at managing my time.'

Driving your own agenda

How you manage your time has serious implications. When time gets on top of you, poor results are close behind. The accompanying stress is also likely to affect your health and relationships, as well as your effectiveness at work or in anything you do. Your company's number one priority might be the customer, service quality, or the bottom line. But before any such worthy goals can be achieved, you need to put:

♦ yourself
♦ your health and sanity
♦ your personal development
♦ your goals and aspirations

at the top of any agenda.

A so-called empowering company will no doubt claim to value its staff highly. If this is more than the usual rhetoric, fine. But the best sort of empowerment is *self-empowerment.* That's where you drive your own agenda, especially in the way you use your time.

Being 'in control' is largely a matter of perception. One person feels in control, acts accordingly and achieves a lot in a limited time. Another person might have far fewer actual external demands, but quickly caves in and can do no more than fire-fight. This is not so much a matter of tools and techniques, as state of mind and belief.

The sort of agenda you need to set for yourself involves creating new empowering beliefs and drawing upon the winning, productive states of mind you have known in the past. Start writing the agenda for what you want to achieve, and accept that you have the inner resources to bring it about.

Slick systems

Some people and most organisations are preoccupied with systems. Many solutions to the time dilemma are based on proprietary diary-type or other recording systems. It's no secret that such products produce healthy profit margins, apart from the accompanying training. It is little wonder, then, that objectives are clouded and that systems or gadgets – essentially tangible 'things' – are central to the solutions offered. Still less wonder that, by and large, and certainly in the longer term, the 'systems' do not work.

The evaluation of such systems, however, is also suspect. Let's face it, who will admit to spending a lot of money on the wrong car, or an inferior toaster? And in the same way who will admit to making an unwise investment in a proprietary system for managing time? For many, a time management device of some kind, such as a filofax or personal organiser, is a badge of office, just like a mobile phone and bulging briefcase.

Good money for bad

Of course there are those who are very much at home with these organising systems. But the chances are they were pretty organised to start with, compared with most of us. Proprietary time management systems might add incremental benefits, but represent 'good money for bad' if they are not based on sound thinking and changed habits.

As well as setting your own agenda to include state of mind and belief, the right-brain approach goes on to include sound thinking and changed habits. Fundamental changes call for more than proprietary systems, or indeed any *external* antidote. The 'systems' you need to employ concern your:

◆ beliefs
◆ attitudes
◆ and every aspect of your behaviour.

These are the stuff of *life* management. Fortunately, these internal, neurological 'systems', once understood and harnessed, are infinitely more effective than any external systems or devices.

Where have all the minutes gone?

Most proprietary systems are based on one key principle of orthodox time management training. The idea is very simple: *you have to find out where your time has gone.* This usually involves keeping meticulous diary records in slots of a few minutes each. This personal time record should then show what has to change. But, more than that, it usually reveals some hard-to-bear facts. You are not just incompetent and ineffective in your job, but lazy, self-centred, not 'directed', and perhaps a poor spouse and parent to boot.

There are serious flaws in this principle of self-management and the methodology used to right it. The process is in some cases supposed to be carried out over a period of several weeks to give a good, representative classification of how your time is spent. This chore will often be the last straw. The poor, overworked time manager is still wondering what mental lapse brought him away from the office for two days in the first place. The fact that your daily time allocation is a 'five minute investment' does not help if you forget to do it on day four, or sooner. You may then have to start all over again or (apparently) the system, based on the 'know where your time went' principle, is invalid. Remember, of course, that you don't even begin to apply the techniques and systems until you have faithfully carried out your self-evaluation, upon which your new behaviour needs to be based.

For most humans of the time-pressured, disorganised kind, such a methodology is not feasible. It will take a time management miracle just to get the recording and analysis carried out. Needless to say, such people's lives are not imbued with such miracles.

There are short cuts to the process, especially for senior managers, such as delegating the whole process to your secretary. But these do not have the same impact, and may well cover up or exacerbate the real productivity problem. Time management experts say that managers can hardly believe what they have actually spent their time on, having carefully recorded it personally. So there is little chance of believing anybody else, especially if the True Record damns you as a gossiping, office-wandering, idle waster.

Even more fundamentally, we are all highly subjective in the way we 'classify' what we spend our time on. For example, one person might allocate great chunks of time to 'training staff', or 'motivating staff' or 'explaining task'. But demotivated, confused subordinates are aware of no such activity. Such time allocation is in the mind of the manager.

These flaws partly explain the universal levels of failure and frustration in the struggle with time, and the systems designed to harness it.

A *different approach*

I began to take a different approach to time recording. If someone told me I was only spending 30 per cent of my time on productive work, I naively believed them. After all, you don't argue with the teacher and get away with it. And in any case it had a ring of truth. I could then immediately start working on what to do about my problem, rather than disprove, over three months (if I could find the time), what is supposed to be a universally known fact. Who was I to dispute the fact that we are all inveterate time wasters?

> If you insist on detailed time sheets, use your common sense and design a system that suits your circumstances.

Remember the danger of distorting hard 'facts', and the subjectivity of any such self-evaluation process. Otherwise join the club and accept the fact that there is room in your life for a massive improvement in your use of time without an itemised listing to prove it.

Received wisdom

A heading in one book reads 'You waste more than 97 per cent of your time'. My reaction: Let's not waste any more. Tell me what I have to do. Don't make me feel worse than I do already.

'Eliminate everything that isn't profitable' and 'think profit' are other examples of time management received wisdom. These injunctions are so plausible that we tend to swallow all their implications. But the reason why most managers want to get control of their time and lives is to be able to spend time doing the things they want to do – the things they *enjoy* doing. And any straw poll will reveal that the sorts of things they have in mind are the intangible, quality aspects of life, and not 'profit' or other measurable outcomes. In fact, we are motivated by pleasure and the benefits we perceive in reaching any goal.

Negative injunctions like 'eliminate', however 'sensible' don't go down well with the unconscious part of the human mind.

You will learn later about the important 'drivers' in your

life, and how these dictate your output in relation to time available.

In writing this book I have made an assumption: that you already accept there is plenty of room for change and improvement. If my assumption is right, you will save lots of time and effort that you can divert to other things that are more pleasurable than filling in time sheets.

Delegation

'Delayering' has eliminated many of the people you were always supposed to delegate work to (but didn't, for whatever reason). But delegation is not so much to do with the number of management layers or structure, nor the skills of the individual manager (who covered the subject on his or her very first management course) as with the manager's attitudes and beliefs. These are the factors that repeatedly have the greatest impact on behaviour.

Management means taking responsibility, including responsibility for work delegated. And that includes taking blame for failure as well as credit for success. So just for starters:

◆ fear of failure
◆ the feeling of a loss of control
◆ insecurity of all sorts

all come into the situation.

Under- or over-delegation is about good or bad management rather than time management. One good reason for delegating is more powerful than a string of excuses why you don't. For instance, what *motivates* the manager who delegates (or doesn't delegate)? Whether you delegate or not, and whether you have 50,000 or five staff reporting to you, you can still have a personal time problem.

What and how to delegate requires some analysis. You need to think in terms of *parts* – of the 'problem', or issue. And breaking things down into parts (in this case, eg, what you can delegate, to whom you can delegate) is the orthodox, left-brain way of thinking. 'Insightful' answers, on the other hand, are usually associated with a more holistic, or right-brain view.

However, the parts do not always contain the solution. Each of us is a total person, with a life outside work. Real problems tend to be holistic, with many aspects to them. Neither their causes nor their solutions are black and white. For example, more often than not it is the conflict between work and non-work that creates the big time problems and accompanying stress.

> Even at work, the best delegators start with a clear understanding of their goals and problems – they can see the trees and the forest, the detail and the big picture.

Delegation is not just a management technique, and is certainly not a panacea. It has to have a basis of good judgement. Sometimes it will be an instinctive part of the pre-holiday 'solution' we referred to earlier. At other times it will be a more conscious, long-term investment in other people who, sooner or later, have to be trusted with responsibility. Either way, it has to become integral to your fuller personal strategy for achieving what you want. Tackling only part of the problem – be it planning, delegating, the equipment, the boss – cannot reflect a holistic view of you as a unique, total person, working and living in your own unique situation.

How you think

How many times have you heard 'Managing your time is about managing yourself'? That's sounds like sound advice, but how do you do that? Mastering time is to do with how you think, your attitudes and beliefs. It concerns the habits, orchestrated subconsciously, that rule so much of our waking day. Ingrained thinking and behaviour patterns that have been rehearsed and fine-tuned over the years make most of us remarkably ineffective (doing the wrong things) in the most efficient manner (in the right way).

New thinking habits

So we need new thinking habits. Habits that work. And that requires know-how, as well as the standard brain upon which we can all draw. For instance, there are specific ways to change any belief that has outlived its usefulness, and you will learn how to do that in Chapter 4. More positively, I will explain in the next chapter how you can use your natural creativity and empowering beliefs to confront the unique problems and situations you face.

- ◆ By starting on the inside, and on the neglected right side of your thinking 'control room', you are most likely to see big changes.
- ◆ The deeper you draw on your mental resources, the more lasting and radical the changes will be. As we have seen, that involves the unconscious part of your thinking.
- ◆ Shortage of time is no barrier for these resources when they are used to the full. The best time managers are thinkers as well as doers.

Top achievers – people who get results – don't see *time* as the problem anyway. Rather, the problem is about personal productivity and output.

Positive thinking and self-belief

Most time management problems relate to how we see or perceive things – how we think. Does an optimistic person, for instance, act differently from a pessimistic person when it comes to wise use of time? Of course they do. And what about the difference between a positive and a negative view of things generally? We must have learned something from a generation of 'positive thinking'.

What of self-beliefs? Is there any self-belief that is not self-fulfilling in some way? So where does that leave those who readily confess 'I am pretty disorganised', 'I usually miss deadlines', 'I lose all track of time', 'I get bogged down with detail', 'I can't concentrate'? How damaging are these personal beliefs and labels to our actual performance? What of the effect of other negative 'beliefs' which lurk below the surface, that we are not even conscious of, and their sinister effect on our performance? Such beliefs are at the very core of self-management and time management.

Some take the view that attitudes and beliefs are out of bounds. 'That's just the way I am' is a typical response. In fact, you can replace redundant, unwanted beliefs with empowering ones by doing simple exercises later in the book.

Try it now	How do you see yourself as a manager of time? What do you believe about yourself that will affect your behaviour and performance? Tick which of the following statements apply to you.

- ◆ I am pretty disorganised.
- ◆ I often miss deadlines.
- ◆ I often lose all track of time.
- ◆ I can't concentrate for long.
- ◆ I have difficulty saying 'no'.
- ◆ I start jobs all right but am not so good at finishing them.
- ◆ I am loath to trust others with important work.
- ◆ There are jobs in the home I have meant to do for months.
- ◆ I would like more time to develop new interests.
- ◆ I have several unfulfilled ambitions.
- ◆ I have not got the right balance between home and work.
- ◆ I would like more time to myself.
- ◆ I have let people down in the past.
- ◆ I feel stressed quite often.
- ◆ I do not have the energy I need to cope.
- ◆ I sometimes forget important things.
- ◆ I would like to put more time into keeping fit.
- ◆ I would like to spend more time with my children/ grandchildren/spouse.
- ◆ I have felt the physical strain of too much work.
- ◆ Life sometimes seems like a treadmill.
- ◆ Things are worse than they were five years ago.
- ◆ I need a holiday.

Having ticked these off honestly, decide for yourself whether there is room for improvement, and whether a new approach is worth going for. This is a very time effective exercise – it takes two minutes rather than two months to know whether you need to develop your time management skills, and how fundamentally you need to change.

Add to the above list others that come to mind. It may also help to rank these beliefs. Decide which are the most problematic, or disempowering, and which require special attention.

This exercise will help you to identify and take responsibility for the areas of your life that need to change. Later you will work further on your specific short-list of self-beliefs or 'time problems'.

A personal matter

Where does this right-brain approach to time management take us? Certainly not to slick systems, or even sound principles like delegation, but right back to you as an individual – how you think, what you believe, the state of mind you are in. It doesn't stop at your role as a manager, club secretary or housewife. It concerns what you are as well as what you do. You might move to another job next week, or decide to become self-employed, but it is only yourself – your skills, habits and beliefs – that you will take with you, not your role.

Leaders who control their time

Whatever needs to change in your surroundings and circumstances, the biggest changes – and certainly the first ones to make – happen on the inside.

> Time management is personal management.

In my research into top leaders one of the clearest findings was that these people can move from company to company and success follows them. Nor do they crumple if a couple of layers of management have to be taken out. They are not locked into either a management role definition or a particular corporate structure. They also happen to have cracked the main time problem, focusing on outputs rather than inputs. Although we all might benefit from time to time from 'being in the right place at the right time', real success lies with what goes on inside the individual rather than outside.

Success characteristics

The success characteristics of top business leaders give us

plenty of clues about managing time. Delegation, for example, so prominent in the management textbooks, hardly figured in my 200 interviews with chairmen and chief executives. Nor did planning, in any formal sense, or monitoring, or the classic management functions. Planning became *self*-planning, and control *self*-control. Delegation was simply a function of any senior position in the organisation. The leadership dimension was in knowing what and when *not* to delegate. The same subjective judgement pervaded every self-management issue.

◆ The good news about self-management is that change is within your control.

◆ Time management is a highly personal matter. The secret is in the way you think. How you use your brain.

More specifically, you need to tap into the creative, but largely unconscious part of your thinking. Top leaders, I found, take this approach (although mostly unknowingly – which is what makes it so effective) rather than conforming to textbook time management rules. 'Gut feelings', and a host of other right-brain kinds of mind feats, have at last come out of the closet. It's all right to be intuitive and creative and it doesn't mean you are a lazy timewaster. It does mean you are using your brain more effectively.

Beyond positive thinking

Pareto's law

One principle of management theory we can draw upon in our search for better time management is the ubiquitous 80/20 rule: that 80 per cent of our effort produces just 20 per cent of the results. And vice versa: we spend just 20 per cent of our time producing 80 per cent of our outputs. It is an uncannily universal phenomenon. For example, 80 per cent of a company's customers provide some 20 per cent of sales revenue, and conversely just 20 per cent of them account for a full 80 per cent of revenue. Pareto's 80/20 rule, as it is known, has done a lot for time management and to this day is worth a dozen techniques (see Figure 2).

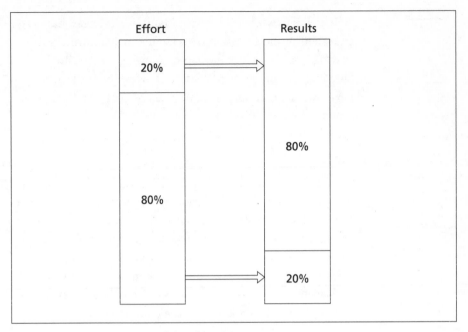

Fig. 2. Pareto's law.

Positive thinking

A positive mental attitude can do wonders for your time management. But how can you adopt such an attitude, other than for the brief period after reading the book or attending the motivational seminar? Positive thinking just seems to work for positive thinkers. And, in any event, it is hardly the stuff of management *science*.

The secrets of a positive attitude belong in the mind. That's where the mysteries of motivation and human excellence are born. And the human mind remains relatively untapped and incomprehensible. As one scientist put it, we know little more about the human brain than if it were stuffed with cotton wool.

However, based upon even a basic understanding of how the brain operates, we now have ways to change our:

◆ feelings
◆ perceptions
◆ and behaviour

if we care to.

The creative role of the right-brain, in particular, has been undersold in the explosion of 'scientific management' and analysis. This book fills the gap in applying right-brain thinking, and the principles and techniques of NLP (neuro-linguistic programming) to time management (see Further Reading for more on NLP).

In two minds

So where does the right-brain come in? The left- and right-sides of the brain work in very different ways. How we think or perceive issues will therefore depend upon which side we tend to use most – our brain *dominance*. More specifically, our attitudes, perceptions and behaviour will relate to the way we *balance* our thinking between the two brain hemispheres.

Sometimes they seem to be in conflict, such as when you declare: 'I'm in two minds.' We can't always reconcile detail and analysis, for instance, with the bigger picture, or we feel strongly about something without having any logical basis for our feelings. On other occasions heart and mind seem to be in harmony, and intuition – albeit usually with hindsight – turns out to be perfectly logical. Most of us are aware of having intuitive 'knowledge' (knowing without knowing how you know), even though we cannot describe it or understand it in any logical way. Paradoxically, intuition, gut feelings, and insights – all associated with right-brain thought processing – can be important factors in how we *control* our time and our lives.

Winning ideas

In many cases the insight that comes from the creative right brain can solve a time management, or indeed any other problem, in a way that ordinary logic cannot. A single good idea, for instance, might mean halving the time it takes to do a task, or even eliminating the task altogether. This seems to be what happens in the productive 'flow' times I have already described. A winning idea might come when showering or driving to the office, or during some apparently unrelated activity. Without such insight the task will remain firmly in an already overstretched schedule. Unfortunately, an unresolved problem usually precedes new and bigger problems, and will add to an already bulging in-tray.

Such insights are a feature of personal excellence and achievement. This applies in both work and leisure situations. Sadly, such insights are all too rare. This is not because they are reserved for the special few, but because we tend to both undervalue and underuse this side of our thinking. Paradoxically, such unconscious thinking is within the reach of every one of us. Thankfully, it requires standard brain hardware. You just need to use your brain in a different way and more fully.

Sleeping on it

Adopting a right-brain approach can be as easy as it is enjoyable. New perspectives on all kinds of familiar situations can dramatically increase your output and the amount you can accomplish in the time you have. Have you ever found that sleeping on a problem, for example, turned out to be a better time management policy than mentally grinding away at the matter, and perhaps making a precipitous decision before one was needed?

> Like gut feelings and the occasional 'eureka', sleeping on a problem, or incubation, is a passive but indispensable part of your brain functioning.

For immediate purposes, it is a feature of the 'system' that brings productivity and helps to solve the time 'problem'. This is another example of the 'no effort principle'. Put simply, you can marshal sleeping time to help you in your waking life.

New perspectives

The importance of the mind generally in behaviour and achievement is well accepted. But *how* we think is especially important, in particular the way we focus on a problem, sleep on it, get insights and intuitions, rationalise and manage our time. We all use both sides of our brain, more or less all the time, of course. There is constant communication between the hemispheres, but we usually have a dominant side. In the western world this is the verbal, logical, analytical left side. This happens to be the side that favours logical, systematic solutions, which the left side designs in the first place. It also tends to follow patterns of thinking from the past, whatever their relevance to the present situation. It forms:

◆ mindsets
◆ preconceptions
◆ and all manner of personal beliefs.

Your left-brain/right-brain preference

You may be interested to know whether you have a bias towards the left or right side of your brain. The simple exercise in Figure 3 will give an indication. Just tick one side or the other – not both. Miss both out if you cannot make your mind up, but do attempt each question. Choose the one that instinctively fits best.

Add up each side, and deduct the lower total from the higher one – this will give an approximation of your left-brain/right-brain bias. You will see from your score whether either side seems to be dominant. It is only likely to be significant if there are at least three or four points either way.

This does not tell the whole story by any means. If you tick a left box it does not indicate how strong your bias is, just whether there is one. Nor does it indicate *how much* you use either side of the brain, just a bias one way or the other. But more importantly, it does not reflect the fact that sometimes you might rely heavily on feelings, at other times heavily on logic. Nevertheless, a simple exercise like this can make you think about how you think – and this is the value.

Most conventional time management thinking can be described as left-brain. Indeed it is this side of the brain that is associated with awareness of the passing of time, being the conscious part of our thinking. Most of the suggestions in this book concern using the right brain *more fully*. That means harnessing the creative, unconscious part of your thinking. (If you want to explore your brain preference see *The Right Brain Manager*, details in Further Reading.)

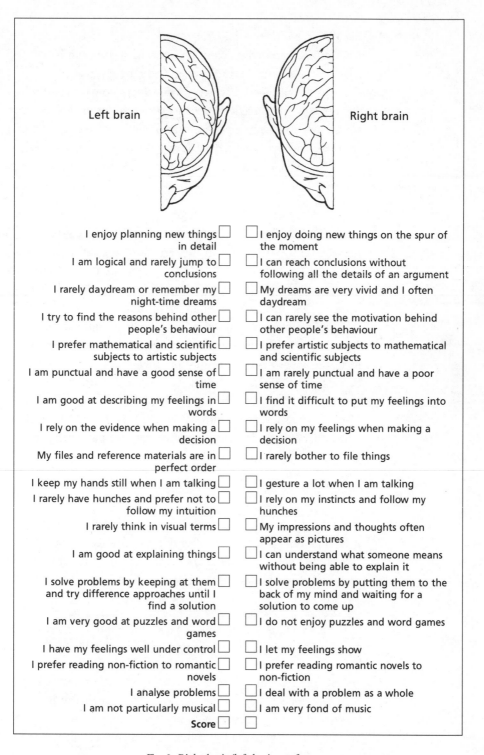

Fig. 3. Right-brain/left-brain preference.

In search of personal excellence

A lot of our knowledge about the working of the brain is relatively new. Much has not yet filtered through to affect everyday management practice. This includes how we manage our time. Where these ideas are being used in business, they are more likely to be applied to areas associated with special creativity, such as new product development or tackling strategic issues 'laterally', or used as a new approach to problem-solving.

180 degrees

The ideas I shall put forward turn some existing thinking round a full 180 degrees, but they are based on well-researched and increasingly popular approaches to how we think. They draw upon many years of experience of working directly with overstretched managers at all levels, in industry, commerce, and the public sector, and countless discussions in seminars and workshops. I also draw on more recent and extensive research involving more than 150 of the chairmen and chief executives of major British plcs (see *Think Like a Leader*, Further Reading). So as well as the ideas being based on the experience of real managers – thousands of them – I have drawn from the best leadership models to be found. It has been a search for personal rather than corporate excellence.

Action

Everything I cover in this book has to be turned into action if it is to be of use. If you have not done so already, go back and tick off any belief statements on the list earlier in the chapter, or spend two minutes checking whether you have a left- or right-brain preference in the way you think.

> This book is about you. That's where the answer to personal time management lies.

Indulge yourself and be ready to see yourself in a much better light where necessary. As you read on, allow yourself to be motivated to accomplish much more, to take control over what you want to achieve, and to put time in its place. Open your mind to a better way.

A compelling inner goal will continuously direct your behaviour towards achieving it.

Inputs, Outputs and Goals

T ime itself need not be a problem. If you can eliminate certain tasks, for instance, then double your output on those that remain (in the way that all of us are capable of), time will have taken care of itself. Your 'problem' might be what to do with the time you save or create. It's what you achieve or don't achieve in the time available that is important.

Within certain margins, we all have the same overall time available to us. The big differences in individual performance concern what we achieve. It's about our performance – the results against which we are measured, our outputs.

There is no doubt that people who have clear goals tend to produce more than those who don't really know what they want.

> Goal-orientation is a key factor in success of almost any sort, whether it is to do with material goals or less tangible quality-of-life goals. It applies equally in personal and corporate life.

If you know where you want to be, it is possible to find a strategy to get you there. If you don't, even the best strategy is futile.

Focusing on outputs

Thinking only in terms of achieving goals or outputs might sound like an efficient, industrious way to live – but boring. However, this implies a narrow view of what goals can be. A complete Sunday to yourself, for example, sounds to me like a reasonable outcome to aim for. Such a goal might contribute towards freedom and independence, peace of mind or some other achievement that your free Sunday represents. It is a quantifiable achievement. You *created* it. It's an output along that road towards the goal you call 'peace of mind'.

Weeks of overtime working or attempts at delegation, and any other use of your time that do not achieve your desired outcome, are just *inputs*. Whether they are efficient or inefficient, inputs that don't get you your Sunday off, or the peace of mind – or whatever – that time off promises, are misdirected. They are ineffective. Put bluntly, they are a waste of time.

So we first have to:

◆ Establish the *outputs* we want to achieve – including those we don't presently accomplish because of the 'shortage' of time.

◆ Know what we would or could achieve if it were not for the 'time problem'.

◆ Differentiate these desirable outputs from the many inputs that go towards achieving our goals – 101 things that fill our time but have little real effect on what we accomplish.

All this affects how we use our time. What if you decide that a different output, or goal, will suit your purposes equally well? And you can achieve it in less time? Maybe you want to do a course of study and gain some skill, but are not bothered about a formal qualification to show for it. The chances are you will achieve your goal, without exams and the stress that accompanies them, more quickly and pleasurably. That doesn't stop you from going on to gain a qualification later, but why put in time and effort if you are not achieving exactly what you are after?

A bit of ingenuity

The time saved can be used to achieve other goals, in other pleasurable ways. With a bit of ingenuity you may be able to arrange to do things you enjoy rather than things you hate, and still achieve your outcome. Even if you don't 'save' time, you will have created some *pleasure* in choosing your goals more precisely. And, in the longer term, that's what worthwhile goals are about anyway.

When you think in output terms, you need to think about achieving specific, measurable goals. That means a certain discipline in the way you think before you do anything. If you have a report to produce, for example, the report is your output, rather than the information gathering process, planning, discussions and checking that went into it. These are inputs. Of course your report will have be of a certain quality. Just any old report would not be a satisfactory output. But even a low quality report is better than having excelled in your discussions and research yet having failed to produce the report.

> Concentrating on your end result is fundamental for motivation while you work, as well as final achievement.

The visualised goal attracts you, and motivates your behaviour towards it.

A critical factor

Given a clear goal, you can then consider the most effective and efficient way to achieve it – the inputs that are needed. Time itself may be a critical factor. That is, you are short of it, and cannot replace it with other resources like money, people or energy (this may apply, for instance, in companies who can buy time [man hours] and convert it into productivity, and more money). Every minute you save can be used to do other aspects of your goal, and thus increase your chances of success. Just as units of money can buy you anything you want, so units of time are of universal value – you can convert them into other things, including back into money. 'Other things' are either things you should have done in the first place but were too busy, or maybe things you would prefer to be doing given the freedom and time. Whether you increase your chances of achieving a certain goal by making better use of your time, or free up spare time for other goals, you have got the better of time by achieving outputs better. In any event you need clear goals.

If you are not clear about what you want, you might spend precious time, whether efficiently or inefficiently, achieving something you did not want. Such time is lost *forever*, and to no purpose. You have forfeited the outputs you really wanted.

Your opportunity cost

Viewed in this way, every minute you spend has an 'opportunity cost' – the benefit you have forgone by not using the time for something else. If you spend your time doing the decorating, you cannot clear the work backlog you brought home. If you spend time with your children, you are not spending it on some important reading you meant to do. Like the Pareto 80/20 rule, opportunity cost is a key principle in time management. It specifically directs us towards outputs (that we value) rather than inputs (which simply cost us).

So it makes sense first to decide what you will have to forgo (like learning German, or a re-landscaped garden, or a tidy desk) in place of something else. Better still, decide what you don't want in any event (like, perhaps, being an expert on television soaps), and you will add time value instantly.

Getting your goals into order

In thinking about outputs rather than time inputs, you will have to think about your goals – at least sufficiently to identify them. If you do this you will know, for example, what you *don't* need to spend any time on because it is not achieving any goal. Things you don't want to achieve don't 'qualify' as goals. They need have no place in your life, and should not take up your time. That's important self-knowledge if you want to do anything worthwhile with your life.

Identifying a list of goals is just a crude start. You need a pecking order that reflects your personal values. Put simply, because our time has a cost (an *opportunity* cost), it's got to provide value. And you decide on value – what a particular output is *worth* to you compared with another. For example:

◆ Where do family goals fit in with career goals?
◆ What about social commitments?
◆ What about developing yourself and achieving what you want personally?
◆ How do you reconcile short-term, urgent demands on your time with what is obviously wise to do when seen in the longer term?

Your personal hierarchy of goals

In practice we each have a hierarchy of goals or outcomes, similar to that shown in Figure 4.

1. At the top of the hierarchy we might seek the outcome of happiness, contentment, or fulfilment – 'life goals'.

2. At the next level we might aim for financial independence, good health and other fairly high level interests.

3. To support these worthy outcomes more specific *subsidiary* outcomes will be needed, further down the hierarchy. These might include getting a better job or a higher salary, getting a better house, getting physically fit, doing things with the children, learning a language, or whatever. These are more easily definable than abstract life goals, but might still be measurable in quality rather than quantity terms.

4. Further down the hierarchy we will have to be even more specific. For instance, goals at that level might be:
   - get a mortgage
   - get accepted on a course
   - write to Mary
   - get some new computer software
   - buy the material to fix the garage roof.

5. At the lowest level our outcomes resemble the familiar daily or weekly 'to do' list.

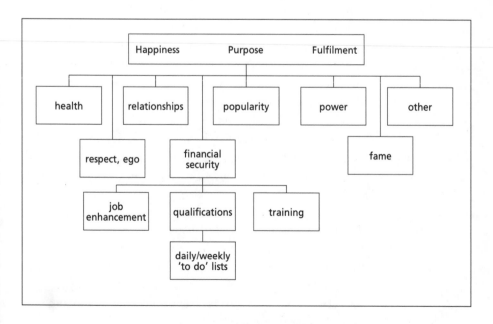

Fig. 4. Hierarchy of goals.

Higher-level goals tend to be longer term. They drive all the lower-level desires and goals, and are the *purpose* of what we do. The advantage of getting your hierarchy of goals onto paper is that you have the basis upon which to decide how best to spend your time. Having defined your outputs, it is immeasurably easier for you to think about appropriate inputs to achieve them.

Mixing and matching your goals

Another advantage of identifying your goals in this way is that you can see how they interrelate, both as lower-level goals contributing to bigger ones, and to goals at the same, competing level. In either case, goals may be complementary or in conflict.

For example, a main outcome of better health might conflict with another of career advancement, which has lower-level goals that will demand lots of your time in sedentary work. Similarly, an outcome concerned with a better family life might conflict with an otherwise reasonable goal of getting professional qualifications, with all the investment of time that involves. So your hierarchy of goals identifies outcomes, and can provide a checklist for you to decide on the pecking order.

By doing such an exercise you might well eliminate whole areas of how you now spend your time. Some goals might be strengthened, as you realise they are contributing more to your life goals than others. You might decide, for instance, that the better health goal will contribute more to contentment, on balance, than will the career one. Or you can change aspects of the career goal so that it fits better, and adds to rather than detracts from other goals like health and self-development. The point is that by not doing what doesn't give you what you want (i.e. constitutes a goal or output), there is no cost or pain. You decide to use your time in achieving things you really want.

Try it now   Have a go at creating your own hierarchy of goals. This should be a fascinating and self-revealing exercise, but you will need to invest some time. Use the illustration in Figure 4 as a guide if you wish, but remember that your goals are unique to you. This personal hierarchy can be extended downwards to almost any level of detail.

Here are some ways in which the process in the exercise above will be of help:

◆ You can decide whether your outcomes – conscious or unconscious – are still valid and are serving you today.
◆ You can amend your goals so that they do not operate in conflict, thus saving time and effort.
◆ You can see whether there are other better (more enjoyable, more rewarding, quicker, easier) ways to achieve higher-level goals.
◆ You will have a blueprint against which to measure everyday activities, to-do lists, and to differentiate between important and urgent.
◆ You will be motivated towards longer-term goals by seeing the big picture of your life.
◆ You may identify purposes or intentions that you may have been pursuing unconsciously, but which you can achieve in a better (quicker, more pleasurable, etc) way.

Outcomes are central to achievement, and thus to managing your time. If you fail to achieve certain goals, you have lost all the time you spent on them. Given your initial choice of outcomes, anything that might increase your success hit rate will thus improve your use of time. If you achieve all your goals, rather than half of them, you have achieved twice as much for the time you have spent.

> You can double your time effectiveness without doing anything more efficiently or having to improve technically – simply by putting your time into achieving the things you want rather than things you don't want.

You can then go further, diverting your time to things you really enjoy, thus getting more pleasure in *working towards* your goals, as well as the pleasure of achievement. Let's say that somehow your garden has been pushed to the bottom of the queue, but you love gardening. By not wasting your time on other abortive work expending time and other resources like money and energy – with no outputs to show for it – you can switch to the gardening you enjoy. Where some tasks are compulsory because they earn the money to pay the bills, it is

even more important to achieve these time-efficiently, and with
some pleasure. Otherwise you will finish up on a treadmill of
living just to work, until you are too old to do the things you
were really working towards.

Testing your outcomes

There are some well-tried rules to apply to outcomes, or goals,
to increase your chances of success, before you even begin to
consider the inputs needed to achieve them. These are tests to:

◆ clarify your goals
◆ make them more specific
◆ and better fitted to your resources.

If you can increase your chances of achieving your outcomes by
common-sense principles, you will release lots of time you now
spend abortively. You will gain further time still as you become
more efficient at what you do to achieve your chosen goals.

These tests apply mainly to the lower levels of your
hierarchy of goals, and you will quickly see why. They are
logical, common-sense tests, which you can apply using right-
brain insight and creativity, rather than in a mechanical way.
When you apply the tests to your goals, try applying them in a
creative way, amending your outcomes in the process, and
recognising the effect of the self-beliefs you have already
identified. If you have not already completed your hierarchy of
goals, stop now to think of a few specific goals, and apply the
tests to them mentally as you read on.

Are my goals specific?

Just writing your goals down, of course, will force you to be
more specific. But keep asking yourself: 'What exactly do I
want?' If you want to learn a foreign language, for example,
decide at what level and for what purpose. Do you just want a
better job, for instance, or do you really want to be in a
different kind of work, perhaps in a different line of business?

A high-level goal, like 'I want to be happy', will beg
obvious questions about what it means (to you) to be happy,
and what goals, if accomplished, would constitute happiness.

This will force you to re-examine your hierarchy of goals, if need be extending it downwards into smaller components that you can be really specific about. Usually a strong desire plus some ingenuity can make the flimsiest dream more likely to succeed. If you find it impossible to be specific, the likelihood of achieving your goal is greatly reduced, and the possibility of spending time fruitlessly is increased. Having been specific about a task you want to accomplish, why not give yourself a deadline?

◆ To fulfil the specific criterion, ask yourself: 'What exactly, and by when?'

Will I have reasonable control over whether I achieve my goals?

If success depends on someone else, your chances of a satisfactory outcome are reduced significantly. If you are one of a team, for instance, you may not be able to significantly influence the results of a group task or project. If you are the team leader, however, you will have a greater chance of success.

In a work situation you may not have any choice, of course. On the other hand you may be able to negotiate before you take on a task, when there is at least the chance of rearranging resources and influencing things. It is better to use your creativity in this way than, as is more common, in making excuses after the event when you have been on a hiding to nothing. Sometimes, paradoxically, it is worth taking on extra responsibility if authority and resources go with it. You can then rely on your own ability, rather than be at the mercy of others who can influence an outcome.

This test can be applied in many situations. Your goal may concern your children, for instance, and your wishes on their behalf. However well-intentioned your goals for a son or daughter, the final outcome is more likely to be in their control than yours. It might be better to set goals that you can personally fulfil. For example, you might help in some specific way with their education, or get them started in business, or do more activities together. These are things you can do, and together they might well bring about your bigger outcome for your child, or anyone else who is part of your goal hierarchy. This not only fulfils the test of control or influence, but you are well on your way to deciding on the specific inputs – in this case carrying out activities with the child – you need to fulfil your 'proxy' outcome.

◆ Ask, in each case, 'What will I, personally, do to achieve this goal?'

How will I know when I have achieved my goal?

What evidence will you have that you have got what you wanted? In many cases this is easy – something physical will be produced like a report, or reorganisation, or there will be an entry on your bank statement. The bathroom scales and a tape measure can also provide excellent evidence.

In other cases, however, you may have to devise evidence and build it into your outcome, both to give yourself extra motivation and also to make it easier for others to know what you have achieved. This adds healthy pressure from outside, and you are less likely to fall back on excuses if you do not succeed.

The more tangible the evidence, the better. Preferably the outcome should be such that it can be seen, heard and felt internally long before it is achieved in reality. 'Sensory representation' implants a clear goal on the mind, which acts as a further motivator.

At this stage you are still just concerned with 'fixing' goals, and not the means to bring them about. So if you are fitting a new kitchen, for instance, visualise the *end result*, rather than the ups and downs of achieving it. If you are installing some computer software, decide what will be the evidence that the project is complete, and visualise that. Sometimes evidence is external or even formal, but sometimes you have to build in evidence for your own purposes.

◆ Ask: 'How will I be sure I have achieved my goal?'

Are my goals at the right level?

If your goals are too small you might get bored along the way, and you will certainly not work at your peak. On the other hand, if a goal is too big panic can set in, which almost guarantees poor use of your time. So you need to pitch it at the right level, if necessary renegotiating a task that has been given to you by someone else.

A big job can usually be broken down into more manageable chunks. In a similar way, a smaller job can be given a tighter deadline to make it more demanding. We each operate at an optimal level of pressure, and this can affect our productivity and time management. This is where your hierarchy of goals helps. Whilst needing to be highly motivated for each task, you need to be able to see the longer-term benefits if you are to keep going. Each outcome has to make sense at a higher level.

◆ Ask yourself: 'Will I be motivated to achieve this goal?'

Who or what else might be affected?

First check what effect one goal might have on others. Small changes can affect you in an indirect way, and your goals need to be congruent with each other – for instance a career goal and a hobby goal. But you should also check that they are not in conflict with the goals of other people who you would not wish to trample on. Your own career goal, for example, might well affect your partner or your children.

These conflicts might well only operate below the surface – unconsciously – but they will affect your motivation, and the chances of success. So they have to be sorted out before rather than after expending energy on outcomes you really did not wish to pursue. Sometimes only minor changes are needed. For instance you might postpone getting that extra qualification until some other family or work matter has been settled.

In this test a more creative question might be called for: 'If I could have my outcome, at this very moment, how would I act and feel?' Often a simple goal like wanting a factory manager's post will be in conflict with other domestic and social outcomes. There may be downsides, in any event, such as losing a circle of friends, having to make a speech at the Christmas party, taking on new responsibilities, or perhaps moving home. Other people's goals might also be affected, such as those of a partner, child, or aged parent. These factors usually surface when the goal is about to become reality.

◆ Ask yourself: 'What might happen if I achieve this goal?'

Have I got what it takes?

This test is to do with the personal resources you can use in achieving your goals. It is mainly concerned with fairly immutable characteristics, rather than material resources that can be acquired (as another goal, if you wish) or even skills that can be acquired over a period. For most people, a burning desire to be a heavyweight boxer or ballerina might be out of the question if you apply this test. Age is also a personal 'resource' factor. An ambition might be quite achievable as a long-term goal at the age of 30, but beyond the bounds of reason at 60. Having said that, we usually underrate ourselves, and most of us can quote cases where amazing personal handicaps have been overcome in the pursuit of clear goals, apparently despite the age factor.

Although we generally tend to underestimate our ability, in some cases we are the last person to recognise that we do not have what it takes. So for this test in particular you may need to resort to a trusted friend. They can then apply the key question: 'Has he or she really got what it takes?' Usually alarm bells will ring if there is a problem.

If you set yourself worthwhile goals, and habitually achieve them, you will solve the 'problem' of time. You have no doubt heard the saying: 'If you have anything you need doing, give it to a busy person.' The sort of person who achieves a lot can usually take on a lot more and still manage. Setting sound outcomes is vital, and they can be made much more robust by applying these common sense tests, which top achievers apply without thinking.

The logic is simple:

◆ Unless you have goals to work for, you have no measure against which to judge your use of time – or anything else.

◆ If you are working away at goals you do not really want, all of that time could be spent on something you do want to do, or that will at least take you nearer to longer-term goals.

◆ Having set your goals, anything you can do to increase their chances of being achieved will save more time, as you will be involved in fewer abortive inputs.

◆ Tackling your time in this fundamental way means tackling your life, and what you are doing with it.

If you have not already got round to it (time is so short, isn't it?) draw up your hierarchy of goals and apply the tests. Some high-level goals, in the abstract terms in which we usually state them, might fail one or more of the tests. Good health or financial security, for example, might not be specific enough to work towards, or you might need to think about the evidence of having achieved them. But the experience will help you to identify the supporting goals (like reaching a certain weight, paying off the mortgage by a certain date, or having a certain amount in the building society) that will make your high-level life goals a reality. Lower-level goals that get through the tests will bring about your top goals in an effective and more predictable way.

Having drawn up your hierarchy of outcomes, and amended it after applying the tests, you now have a personal profile of outcomes. Various 'evidences' are the outputs you will work towards. This determines what your inputs will be – what you will spend your time on.

Inputs

Anything you do that uses up your time can be classed as an input. It is what you do to achieve your outputs, intentionally or unintentionally, and whether or not you are successful. As we have seen, sometimes these inputs will take you in the wrong direction and do not produce outputs you have decided upon. It doesn't matter how worthy, enjoyable, efficient, or demanding these inputs are. Unless they achieve something you desire, they are literally a waste of time. So it is vital to identify:

◆ first your outcomes
◆ then your quantifiable or observable outputs.

Sometimes we pursue intentions unconsciously. If you feel you have to do something, having given it thought, it is likely that there is some outcome you are trying to fulfil, even though you cannot identify it, or at least express it. For example, you may get sympathy from people who see you patiently struggling. This fulfils the outcome 'I want to be appreciated'. And that's fine, but maybe there are other things you could do (inputs) which would make you more appreciated, or that will fulfil goals you value even more than the (unconscious) goal 'to be appreciated'. You can make up your own mind, but remember that you are handling a unique resource, *your time*. Time used for one purpose cannot be reused for something else.

Examples of inputs and outputs

So far I have simplified the idea of inputs and outputs to make it clear how important it is to differentiate between them. In practice, however, you might need to give a bit more thought to whether a behaviour or activity is one or the other. A report that has to be produced, for example, is an output. But depending upon the situation, a report might be just an input to a bigger task or project, rather than an output in itself. Failure to differentiate between inputs and outputs in different situations accounts for lots of muddy thinking and poor use of time. You often need perspective and insight to know whether you are actually contributing to an outcome, rather than just carrying out an activity, however efficiently.

Getting sales appointments

Using a sales example, let's say that you spend one afternoon each week fixing up sales appointments by telephone. The work you are doing is making telephone calls, but that is not your output, unless you have no responsibility at all for getting appointments and your employer is happy to let you sit telephoning all day with no results. What if you make more calls? You can try that, but it is possible that you might still not get any firm appointments. Or you can improve your technique, changing the words you use and voice intonation. But still, if you don't achieve appointments that can be converted into sales you have achieved nothing according to the company's objectives, and no doubt your own as well.

In this case a little thought will solve the matter. Instead of making your objective a certain number of telephone calls, you could make it a certain number of firm appointments. Obviously you will have to agree on a number, perhaps based on experience initially or what colleagues can achieve. But now, importantly, you are working towards a real output.

Let's say your target is five appointments in the afternoon. *Anything* you do that results in reaching your target is an input related to an output. And changing the nature of your inputs might produce more outputs. You might find, for example, that you are more successful making longer calls – fewer calls but getting more appointments. Or you might find certain words get appointments better than others, even though the conversations are not as chatty as they used to be.

What is almost certain is that by concentrating on successful outputs – what you achieve – *you will get better over a period*, thus becoming more and more efficient in your use of time. If you can get five appointments in an hour, for instance, you have the rest of the afternoon either to make further successful appointments or to do something else to achieve other outputs.

If you think in terms of inputs alone you will have done well to increase your level of telephone calls, even if you only make two appointments. But according to your own and the company's objectives, you will have failed. If you don't recognise this, you are likely to carry on becoming more skilled – more efficient, in fact – at *not producing results*. If you think in terms of outputs, however, you will naturally – without necessarily working harder at all, and by trial and error – learn to achieve worthwhile results.

Creating company outputs

What if you are the salesperson, responsible for making the personal visits, as well as arranging the calls? This changes things – your outputs then become sales. The number of appointments you keep is not a measure of final success. It is the rate at which you can convert them to sales. If you can make sales without appointments, for example, you will surely do so. In this case the salesperson, in making the telephone calls, is not just aiming for a firm appointment, but is seeking to increase the chances of an eventual sale.

However, experience probably shows that appointments are an essential part of the selling process – a partial output towards making the sale. So, for instance, he or she might choose telephone targets differently, or even do preliminary selling work as part of the telephone call, all with a view to making more eventual sales. In this case both telephone calls and appointments are inputs, but are more directly linked to sales outputs, which register as results further up the company hierarchy in the form of profits.

Manageable chunks

Breaking up a goal into smaller component parts is fine, provided that each chunk contributes to the bigger goal. But in the drive to complete a task the ongoing question of whether a desired output is being achieved might well be overlooked. You can be expert at making inputs without achieving worthwhile outputs. And the more time and cost savings that can be identified, with the semblance of activity and efficiency, the more the task takes on its own life outside the mission of either the business or the manager. Miles travelled, visits made and a bulging briefcase are rarely measures of success.

Whose outcome anyway?

Sometimes specific outcomes are an inherent part of your job. If you cannot morally accept them, then your problems are not just to do with managing time. You may be in the wrong job. Or you may be happy with a compromise outcome. Either way, by honestly identifying your personal outcomes you have some choice over what you want, whatever the pleasure or pain involved.

Some 'handed-down' outcomes can be discussed and renegotiated – for example, if they are too demanding or not demanding enough, or do not fit departmental or company goals, but in many cases you will fix your own outcomes. This applies more socially and personally. You can then decide yourself on when an input becomes an output, and what goals are contributing to bigger goals in your hierarchy. That is why your personal hierarchy of outcomes is so important.

The power of an inner image

Sometimes referred to as 'mental rehearsal', or 'future pacing', the technique of *visualisation* has been shown to be beneficial in clarifying goals and increasing the chance of success. Most of us seem to have a goal-seeking tendency, much like a missile keeping track of its target, based on cybernetic feedback systems. By clearly imagining your desired outcome it becomes etched on your brain like an inbuilt goal or target. Visualisation supports goal achievement and can also change your feelings, beliefs and perceptions about a particular situation, activity or outcome.

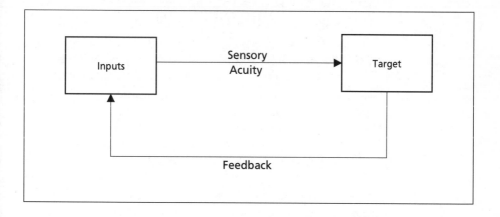

Fig. 5. Cybernetic feedback system.

The principle behind it is simple. The brain does not differentiate between a clearly imagined inner experience and the real thing. This is starkly apparent when you wake from a vivid dream and you are not sure whether the dream or the room you are in is real. By imagining an outcome, we create an internal sense of belief and familiarity – as though it is a real sensory experience. Then we tend to be drawn towards the visualised goal (see Figure 5).

Success seems natural to people who hold a strong visual image of what they want to accomplish. Achieving some sports accolade or other life ambition, for example, is often traced back to a childhood dream. A recurring image of visiting some distant country sooner or later tends to become reality. And the budding managing director seems to live the role long before he or she is appointed.

Using all your inner senses

Visualising pays off in many ways. The visualising process itself, by definition, is a pleasurable one. Mental contemplation of a dream holiday can sometimes be more pleasurable than the real thing – which, of course, is not all within your control. The use of all the inner senses creates the necessary reality. This seems like magic, but the sophistication of the human cybernetic systems is cleverer than magic. Done in a focused, purposeful way, visualising is also positive and constructive – it forms a more powerful motivator than even writing down your goals or stating them out loud, and it actually helps bring about specific goals. The process accounts for the remarkable cases of achievement we meet all the time where no training or external systems are called upon.

> Get into the habit of rehearsing your outcomes mentally – seeing, hearing and feeling them – until they become real.

Repeating this process makes them become familiar, credible, and sooner or later, inevitable. Relaxation is important, and you may wish to do some extra reading or even training to help you.

We all use visualisation techniques naturally. When you make a decision, for instance, you will probably go over the possible scenarios in your mind and settle on what 'feels' right. What we call 'worry' is a negative application, when we clearly envisage the worst that might happen. But the process can be used consciously and positively, to bring about specific outcomes. Having developed the skill, like any other skill, you will have learned how to create your own future. The only limitation is the power of your imagination.

*What you
believe about
yourself is
crucial to what
you do and
what you
achieve.*

CHAPTER 4

Managing Your Self-Beliefs

I t is often said of time management that 'It's not about
managing your time, but managing yourself.' An ounce of
motivation, for example, is worth pounds of systems. In fact,
self-belief has far more impact on how we actually use our
time and what we achieve than a whole portfolio of skills,
systems or even guiding principles. Time management is life
management, and at the heart of the matter are your beliefs
and core values.

This chapter concentrates on *self-beliefs*:

◆ how you can identify them
◆ how beliefs and values fit together
◆ how in turn they affect what you achieve.

You started to identify some beliefs when you rated yourself in
Chapter 2, and the importance of these may have become
more apparent as you tried to rank them. Most of all, I want to
stress how critical self-beliefs can be to every aspect of your life,
and in particular in the way you use your time. In turn, I want
to show the leverage that can be gained by tackling the right
issues – certain key factors that account for outstanding
performance in others and ourselves.

Self-beliefs

A single belief about yourself, such as 'I never seem to finish
things properly' can be uncannily self-fulfilling. It can mean the
loss of great chunks of your time that no personal organiser
system can make up for. Conversely, a simple belief about
yourself such as 'I know how to say "no"', or 'I can solve
anything if I set my mind to it' can multiply what you can
accomplish with your time, as compared with a person with a
more negative belief.

Core values and purpose

Certain personal core values – justice, sincerity, industry, honesty, or whatever – give a sense of direction and purpose, without which most time management tools and techniques are wasted. If the value you place on your family life is higher than that which you attach to your career, for example, all sorts of goals and behaviour will result in line with that value.

> How you spend your time will be broadly determined by your values, even before you start setting specific goals and making out 'to do' lists.

Your goals – where you want to get to, what you want to accomplish, your outcomes – will be built upon, or at least be congruent with, your values and your beliefs about yourself – how you 'see' yourself.

Self-fulfilling spirals

Every pattern of thought – every belief, value, attitude, or feeling – has an effect on what we do with our time and lives. If one morning you feel on form or productive, for instance, the chances are you will do better and achieve more. Equally, a depressed state the next day could render you close to useless in terms of actual output. Neither feeling may have a rational basis. Although a nuisance, these feelings are ephemeral. You can often shake yourself out of negative feelings by getting involved in real activity, which occupies your mind.

Strongly held beliefs and values, however, can have a powerful influence over how we behave over a longer timescale. Some of those self-beliefs you ticked off on the list in the previous chapter may fall into this category. 'I do not seem to have the energy...', for instance, might translate into actual physiological symptoms that both fulfil and further reinforce your belief. Beliefs are powerful. And the more general or all-embracing they are – like 'I am pretty disorganised' – the more areas of your life they will affect in a disempowering way.

By confronting undermining self-beliefs, we can easily double or even quadruple what we might otherwise achieve in the allocated time we all have.

Systems and techniques that do not take into account these aspects of our thinking and behaviour will fail. And they do fail. In a work situation, for instance, harassed managers keep returning to seminars and systems, hoping for something that brings more than incremental, short-term results.

Such methods and training can actually be counter-productive. You start with the common, self-fulfilling belief, 'I can never get organised.' After a week's course and expensive proprietary systems, and no observable improvement, your belief is reconfirmed with a vengeance. It now runs (if you were to express it): 'Having attended the best course and having tried hard to follow the system, there really must be something wrong with me. I am *really* disorganised.'

Ingenious self-justification

There are well-researched bases for this concept of self-fulfilling cycles of belief and behaviour. Common sense and a little personal reflection will usually confirm that unsatisfactory aspects of behaviour into which we lapse are 'justified' by self-beliefs such as 'I'm just not the organised type.' If you like, that belief is sufficient excuse.

Time and effort spent on training can equally be justified. For example, we swear that our output has gone up by 30 per cent and that such-and-such is a brilliant technique – justifying our behaviour as we tend to justify an expensive purchase we have wisely made. But the reality is our actual, unchanged performance. The true result – given the time and effort and a reconfirmation of our negative self-belief – is counter-productive.

How you use your time is too fundamental a matter to be treated with external, 'product' solutions. Change starts on the inside, where there are few opportunities for excuses.

The power of mental habits

The structures and thinking patterns we form in the brain are habits – mental habits that produce attitudes and beliefs, and the behaviour that inevitably follows. However disempowering or even irrational they may be, such habits are familiar and comfortable. They will usually have had some original, long since overtaken, purpose. But you need not be stuck with them. They represent the software programs of your thinking, and can be changed and replaced as you wish.

More positively, these mental habits allow us to live full lives, and survive, without 'thinking' (consciously) too much. Everything, from optimism to shyness, or which shoe you put on first, is a learned strategy, constituting a few million electrochemical neural happenings. The good news is that we can change these habits, or patterns of thinking. We can *control* them, thus changing the behaviour upon which all our outcomes are based. But first we need to identify the disempowering beliefs that interfere with our productivity.

Irrational, diverse and unique

Our thought patterns are as diverse as they are unique. Different things motivate different people. We sometimes talk, for instance, of pressing an individual's 'hot button', or of trying to find out 'what makes them tick'. Similarly, we see the effect of irrational, limiting self-beliefs all around us. 'I'm no good with numbers' probably means that your performance in that area is well below what it should be on the basis of your education and training. A person who believes 'I am good at numbers' will usually have the edge – not least because their confidence means they take opportunities to display their skills, and practice makes perfect.

Don't expect to find any rationale behind your beliefs, especially those about yourself. More positive colleagues will outperform us hands down because of the power of their respective self-fulfilling beliefs, however irrational those may be.

> The best time managers may not boast paper qualifications or high training, but usually ooze simple and powerful belief in themselves and what they can accomplish.

They also know what they are after – the goals we discussed in Chapter 3.

In its starkest form, belief can turn black into white. Its

effects are very tangible: 'I'm ugly', or 'I'm fat' are familiar affirmations that deny what friends and relatives know to be reality, yet can have real and dangerous consequences. These beliefs can – even when uttered in a light-hearted way – control our behaviour and achievement. Each of us is controlled by negative self-beliefs, any one of which is likely to have a bigger impact on our effectiveness than the most sophisticated system or technique. But at the same time each of us is usually the last to identify such beliefs, or to recognise their effects.

Self-beliefs that hinder and help

The list of beliefs that can have a major impact on what we do with our time and what we achieve is endless. We met a few in the previous chapter, but many keep turning up and are spread thickly through the world of management. Here are the sorts of beliefs I refer to:

- ◆ I'm a slow reader.
- ◆ I couldn't make a speech if you paid me.
- ◆ My mind often goes blank.
- ◆ I'm hopeless at remembering names.
- ◆ I'm no good with anything mathematical.
- ◆ I can't spell.
- ◆ I'm always running late.
- ◆ I'm stubborn like my father.
- ◆ I'm not really a healthy person.
- ◆ I'm not mechanically minded.
- ◆ People usually take what I say the wrong way.
- ◆ I can't stand my accent.
- ◆ I've always looked older than I am.
- ◆ I can't draw a straight line.

Each of these is potentially disempowering. The degree to which they hamper your goal-achievement, however, will relate to the goals themselves. If being a good speller is important in what you want to achieve, then a negative view of your ability as a speller will be disempowering. It will prevent you from getting what you want. Similarly, a negative self-belief about remembering names will not do you much service if you are a salesperson, or in a job requiring a lot of interpersonal contact. Whether such self-beliefs are negative or positive, disempowering or empowering therefore depends on your desired outcome.

Having said this, a mixture of negative self-beliefs can lower a person's *overall* self-esteem, and have a debilitating effect on just about everything or anybody they come into contact with. In the extreme, the pathetic 'I'm a loser' becomes an all-powerful life driver.

Try it now

Tick off those beliefs about yourself that apply, as you did in the earlier list. Some may overlap. Add others that occur to you. Then mark any which might hinder you in achieving what you want – that are disempowering. Positive beliefs about yourself are just as powerful in the same self-fulfilling way. Here are some universally empowering beliefs:

◆ I am an optimistic person.
◆ I am enthusiastic about anything I do.
◆ I am a natural goal-achiever.
◆ I always take care of details.
◆ I am open to new ideas.
◆ I am dependable.
◆ I am blessed with natural talents.

These are the sorts of beliefs that will empower you in a whole range of situations, and will again relate to your present goals or outcomes. A role requiring you to see the 'big picture', for instance, will not need the attention to detail that another job might. In this case the belief 'I quickly see the big picture' will tend to be empowering.

Extend the list as long as you can make it. Then, just as in the previous exercise, mark those self-beliefs that are likely to be helpful to you in achieving what you want – that are empowering. Then the rule with positive beliefs is simple: leave well alone, even though their origins may have no more rationale than the negative ones.

The key to managing your time and life better is to identify and change disempowering beliefs, attitudes and values. However unjust or painful the past, and whatever the 'reasons' for your negative self-belief, every moment of your life is controlled by brain software that can be rewritten to your current specification. What you want to achieve, where you want to go, what you want to be – these will determine how you use your time, and whether you fill your life with pleasure or pain.

Thinking strategies

To achieve the outcomes you want you need matching beliefs or thinking strategies. A written life 'mission', supported by monthly written goals and daily 'to do' lists is not enough. You need internal strategies that control:

◆ how you feel
◆ your attitudes
◆ what you believe about yourself
◆ and your core values.

These are just mental patterns, structures, or mindsets – the 'syntax' of how you represent and understand the world.

Further strategies will control your behaviour, what you do – most of it by habit – to bring about your outcomes. Strategies are vital in companies and other organisations. They are even more fundamental to how we behave as individuals. Just as when designing or choosing computer software to do a certain job, it is important to have the right strategies to achieve what you want. If this sounds cerebral, remember that we all run all sorts of strategies anyway. It's just that we are not aware of them and many don't work. Self-management means using our awesomely effective 'system', but to bring about our particular, conscious purposes.

Building on beliefs

You will not get far managing your time without deciding on your outcomes – what you want to achieve. What we do – how we behave – cannot take place in a vacuum. There must be a purpose, based on the firm foundation of our values and self-beliefs.

If you set goals that are not in line with your values, you

may accomplish a great deal, but you will not be satisfied, because you are neglecting the things that matter to you most. At a daily level, you are likely to be busy, but not productive in the way you really want to be. Put another way, you may achieve one goal or outcome – a tangible one, say – but not the 'outcome' of conforming to a belief or value. To keep to your values is another *desire*, just as real, however rarely expressed. And such outcomes, whether articulated or even held unconsciously, tend to be the strongest motivators in all our behaviour. You have to live with yourself.

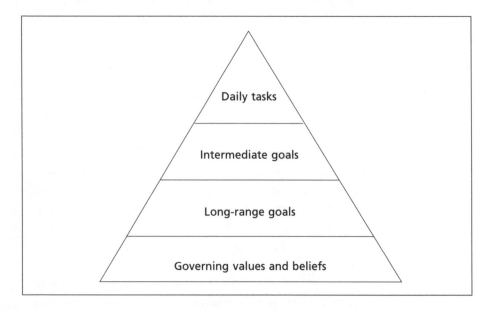

Fig. 6. Values, beliefs and outcomes.

This relationship between values and beliefs and outcomes can be represented by a pyramid, as in Figure 6. Life goals grow out of our beliefs and values, intermediate goals support these longer-term life goals, and our everyday tasks support our intermediate goals. So each item on the ubiquitous daily 'to do' list will find its way not only to a long-term goal, to do perhaps with work or health, but also to values and beliefs like 'I take care of my body' or 'I always finish a job I start.' A single belief might result in many supporting behaviours and these determine what you accomplish with your time. So changing an appropriate belief has more leverage than changing an individual behaviour – there is a better return on the effort you put in.

Pyramid of priorities

There is a need for priorities at each level in the pyramid. If your career comes before your family, for instance, this will affect not just what goals have to be achieved – long-term and medium-term – but also the priority or ranking of the goals themselves, and so on, to affect the nature and order of your daily tasks.

Goal congruence

We have seen that goals and tasks need to be congruent, so that even minor day-to-day tasks fit into a higher long-term goal. In the same way, values and beliefs need to be congruent. This might seem obvious, but there can often be a conflict of values when you are under pressure. Family values may not be congruent with career ambitions, or other worthwhile goals – even charitable ones – that make reasonable time with your family impossible. Or in a business situation, if you are offered a directorship only to be a stooge of the chairman, enhancing his personal voting power, your need for integrity or independence might be in conflict with your search for power or rank. If personal integrity comes first, you might well refuse promotion.

This is where the importance of ranking comes in. If you decide at the start that honesty and integrity (values) come first, you will not be placed in such a dilemma – your decision will be straightforward.

Unconscious 'drivers'

Perhaps less clear is the fact that we are not always conscious of the values and beliefs that drive us. Values, in any event, are likely to have been inherited from family and authority figures. Specific self-beliefs might be traced back to random successes and failures in childhood, but we do not have to give these unconscious values and 'drivers' a mysterious quality they do not deserve. Simply by thinking about and writing down your beliefs and values you will be able to detect the less obvious ones. At the same time, you will probably identify likely conflicts (incongruence, as we have just seen), and decide on your ranking before you are pressured by circumstances.

Inner peace and the bottom line

Discovering what's important to you, and doing something about it, is for the most part simple and practical. Without doubt, achieving the inner peace that most people strive after – especially those who feel at the mercy of time pressures – is what the self-discovery process I am describing is all about. Paradoxically, this intangible inner peace – or however it is described – is the foundation of very tangible achievements. It translates into 'bottom lines' of all kinds, including personal health and happiness. So it's worth getting the foundation of the pyramid right.

Turning knowledge into personal control

Simply being aware of your self-beliefs is more than half the solution. If you are aware of the detrimental effect of some archaic belief, you are likely to make the sort of fundamental changes that are necessary. Or at least you can make a choice about whether to stay as you are. Similarly, if you know just how much ephemeral feelings affect your performance, you will be less likely to continue your slavery to feelings.

You probably know what it is to take control of your immediate feelings for the sake of your children, a sick friend, or when you have to accomplish a demanding task. Using current knowledge about how we think and what the brain responds to, we can go a lot further than this. We can make deliberate, positive changes to our controlling thought patterns. Put simply, we can control how we feel, or even what we believe. For instance, think clearly about a pleasant, motivating memory and note how quickly you can change how you feel. Then imagine how that process could be used when you need to feel on top for an important activity or event.

Relating values and beliefs

The foundation of the pyramid represents values and beliefs. How do these relate? Self-beliefs, both positive and negative, can be all encompassing, like 'I'm always optimistic', or a bit more specific, like 'I'm relaxed when meeting new people', or quite specific, 'I relate well to John'. They have their own hierarchy, in which a higher-level belief is supported by probably several more specific ones. The 'meeting new people' belief, for instance, might slot into a higher belief, 'I can socialise easily', then a still higher one, 'I am a friendly, outgoing person'. But these probably reflect a value about people more generally, such as 'all people are important in their own right.' In other words beliefs about being friendly or respectful are congruent and supportive of lower level beliefs and values. 'I can't stand John', for instance, might not be congruent with your higher self-beliefs.

This relationship partly explains how fixed our overall self-images are. We don't change lifetime values in a hurry – even those that others might consider misguided. A number of different specific beliefs, all probably going back many years, would have to be abandoned or amended in some way before we could begin to change a high-level belief or value. So our beliefs, as well as goals, form their own hierarchy.

Seeing our values in ourselves

Values, such as honesty, self-reliance, sincerity, punctuality, frankness, are just abstractions – words. They are an expression of self-image at the higher levels. Having said this, both values and beliefs can reflect an ideal, rather than a reality, in the sense that we are not always 'honest', 'punctual', or 'frank', although we might like to be. But these are nevertheless the characteristics we value highly, both in ourselves and in others. On the whole, that's the way we 'see' ourselves. We expect to behave in line with these characteristics, and we do. The self-fulfilling spiral of behaviour takes us *towards* rather than *away from* our self-belief, which is further strengthened.

> We act out what we believe, and we interpret whatever we do to fit those beliefs.

A self-image for all seasons

Values are usually thought of as a very short list of characteristics like honesty and sincerity. Self-image, on the other hand, is often used as a single concept. We might say, for instance, that a person has a low or high self-image. This is not helpful, and rarely true, as we each have a unique but long list of ways in which we 'see ourselves' in different situations. A person might have a very high self-image as a sportsperson or as a cook, for instance, but a low self-image academically. Their actual behaviour and achievements, in turn, are likely to exactly match this. They will do well in sport and do badly academically, for no genetic or rational reason, but just because of the belief.

> Overall each of us has a cocktail of beliefs about ourselves, some positive and some negative.

Identifying your self-beliefs

The list below illustrates how our personal beliefs extend to every aspect of our lives. It is not exhaustive by any means, but is based on an actual survey. It shows the areas within which different personal beliefs – probably several – are held. They are also listed in terms of their frequency in the particular survey, but do not let this affect how you identify your own unique values and self-beliefs.

1. Spouse
2. Financial security
3. Personal health and fitness
4. Children and family
5. Spirituality/religion
6. A sense of accomplishment
7. Integrity and honesty
8. Job satisfaction
9. Love/respect for others; service
10. Education and learning
11. Self-respect
12. Taking responsibility
13. Exercising leadership

14. Inner harmony
15. Independence
16. Intelligence and wisdom
17. Understanding
18. Quality of life
19. Happiness/positive attitude
20. Pleasure
21. Self-control
22. Ambition
23. Being capable
24. Imagination and creativity
25. Forgiveness
26. Generosity
27. Equality
28. Friendship
29. Beauty
30. Courage.

Try it now   Now have a go at identifying your own values and self-beliefs –
the bottom level of the pyramid. Use the above categories as a
checklist, along with the earlier illustrations of positive and
negative self-beliefs. It will help if you add a few more words –
maybe a couple of sentences – to explain what each abstract
term means. This will help you to define and clarify each belief,
and also to think about how it relates to others.

Having identified these beliefs and values the next step is to put
them in order of priority.

Putting your beliefs into order

Why is the order so important? Applying Pareto's law, to which
I have already referred, a handful of beliefs will be responsible
for the lion's share of your behaviour, and in turn what you
achieve. So it is as well to isolate and correct any outdated and
disempowering beliefs, choosing the few that are the most
disempowering.

Having said that, sorting out priorities is no easier at this
level than choosing between urgent jobs that demand your
immediate attention. We can, of course, hypothesise about

lofty, longer-term aspects of our personality. But this does not always give a true ranking. Sometimes we have to actually experience something to know how we would react, and what our true values are, such as when choosing between family or career, or the conflicting demands of a child and an elderly parent.

Imagine, for instance, you are left a few thousand pounds by a distant relative. You might have the choice of changing your car to a new model, or taking the holiday you have often talked about with your spouse. There are plenty of other possibilities, of course, but let's say these are the first that come to mind. Your choice will probably reflect your ranking of values – your relationship with your spouse, perhaps, as compared with looking good with the neighbours and work colleagues.

Alternatively, a high value on long-term financial security would probably result in you investing the money to build up a nest egg. If your children's welfare came high on your list of values the money might go towards their education, or a start in business. So your pecking order of both values and beliefs will have repercussions in everyday decisions and actions.

Try it now	Try putting your beliefs in order. Apply your own personal ranking to the list, ignoring, if you can, the existing order. If time is really at a premium, just rank the top half dozen. These (on the 80/20 rule) will have the greatest significance in your life.

Square pegs in round holes

One of the biggest areas of values mismatch is in careers and employment. Hundreds of thousands of people are square pegs in round holes. What they spend most of their lives doing does not reflect their real values nor how they really see themselves. That really is poor use of time – if not the best part of a life. yet we rarely think about what is important, what really drives us, and what life is all about. When we do, miracles of productivity and self-fulfilment can soon follow. One woman who completely switched careers in late life to teach music wrote:

'...everything was fun, from that moment on. Theory classes were fun. Music history was fun. Writing my dissertation was fun. There wasn't a thing that didn't bring me joy in the process of pursuing that course.'

Imagine the difference in the way that woman used her time. Career or even job changes are usually considered out of bounds in time management training. But you cannot compartmentalise your life – time is time, whether spent in work or leisure. Managing your time, or any other aspect of self-development, has to be addressed holistically, and will not be constrained to analytical or 'part' thinking. However, it doesn't follow, by any means, that your job is the problem. A couple of belief or attitude changes on your part might well prove to be the answer. But your job may be the problem. You just have one life, and time that slips through your fingers will never be recaptured.

> Establishing congruence between your beliefs and values, at work, at home, and socially, is at the very foundation of controlling your time and life.

Belief change pattern

We have seen that belief is a big factor in what we do, and in turn what we achieve. According to neuro-linguistic programming, belief – like attitude and feelings – is just a way of thinking, a mental strategy for relating to the world. As we have also seen, beliefs can be both acquired and discarded over time. They can be also be consciously changed.

Try it now

Here is an exercise which will help you to change any belief pattern. You can use it to transform limiting beliefs into deeply felt, empowering beliefs, which will create a sense of self-worth and enable you to master all sorts of situations.

1. Identify a belief you now hold that limits you in some way. For instance, the belief might be 'I'm no good at public speaking,' or 'I'm no good with numbers.' Choose a belief which, if changed, could open up real opportunities for you to achieve more in the next few weeks and months.

2. Identify what you would *rather* believe – that is your 'preferred belief', and state this in a positive form. Check that any change will respect your family, friends and work colleagues (one of the goal criteria in Chapter 3).

3. Now create a label on a sheet of paper for each of six imaginary locations of belief change:
   (i)   Current belief.
   (ii) Open to doubt.
   (iii) Museum of old beliefs.
   (iv) Preferred beliefs.
   (v)   Open to belief.
   (vi) Special or sacred place.

4. Place these labels on the floor as though they are places round an imaginary dinner table.

5. The next thing is to establish some sort of anchor for each of the six labels and locations. As you physically step from one to the other, think of a vivid experience from your life which fits each description. You should easily be able to identify your **current belief** – this is the one you would like to change – and imagine yourself in a situation which illustrates this. Then think of a time in the past when you were **open to doubt** – your belief was not strong, doubts had crept in. The belief in doubt might relate to you and your abilities, another person, or even an ideology. For the **museum of old beliefs**, think back to something that you once held as a belief, but no longer believe is true. You can probably think of several dating back to childhood, but some may have been discarded only recently. Your **preferred belief** is the one you would like to change to. For the moment, you need to *imagine that you believe what you want to believe* – or perhaps what it would be like to be another person who you know holds the desired belief. The **open to belief** label will be anchored by some experience in the past when you were open to believe – that is, you had not yet formed a new belief, but your understanding and the facts of a situation made you open to changing what you then believed. Try to think of an actual situation when you were in this particular state of mind. Finally, for the

special or sacred place, think of a belief that you would never discard – something which is so important that it is, to you personally, almost a matter of life and death. Complete one round of the labels and, in each position, try to vividly recollect a situation and state of mind that illustrates each of the different locations.

6. Standing in the **current belief** location, experience again your limiting belief.

7. Taking this limiting belief with you, step from **current belief** into **open to doubt**, and, recalling the earlier experience of being open to doubt. Notice how you are now doubting that limiting belief.

8. Now take your doubted belief and step into the **museum of old beliefs**. Recollect some old, discarded belief, and feel what it is like to discard your doubted belief and leave it here.

9. Having left that belief behind step into your **preferred belief** location and experience again your **preferred belief**. Imagine yourself fully believing this new belief, and enjoy how it feels.

10. Now physically move on into the **open to belief** location, and feel yourself again being completely open to believing the belief is true. Then take your **preferred belief** and step into the **special or sacred place**. Put your new belief alongside your current sacred beliefs, and make it very important to you.

12. Finish the exercise by feeling your now very special and sacred preferred belief as you step back into the **current belief** location. You will now no longer hold the limiting belief as a current belief. It has been transformed, gently, step by step, into a new belief that will be empowering for you.

You will need to use your imagination to make this technique work. Moving from one physical location to another – however silly it seems – actually helps you to make the transition into each state of mind. You are getting to know parts of you that you are not usually conscious of, and some of the rules for doing this do not sit well with the left, conscious side of your brain. By doing the exercise you will also gain more practice in recalling memories, and in particular feelings. Being able to recognise, recall and use your various states of mind for present purposes is in itself an important skill.

The power of a positive self-image

Having plenty of positive self-beliefs brings about an overall positive self-image. That means you can confront problems and set goals in a positive, expectant frame of mind. You concentrate on what you want to achieve, and the process of doing so, rather than on the many obstacles – including shortage of time – that might get in your way.

It is rare to have a low image in every department of your life. But some areas can be particularly low, and these are the ones you can do something about. With a bit of thought you can check your state of self-image health, see how you rate, and in particular which areas need attention. There are certain characteristics that are usually associated with sound psychological health, self-confidence, a positive approach to life and effective use of time. Words such as 'effective', 'confident', and 'open-minded' are used universally.

Try it now

You can use the following lists of characteristics to measure your own estimate of your worth.

Part 1

Make the statement to yourself 'I am an optimistic person', 'I am a tactful person', and so on down the list, scoring Part 1 as follows:

Never	– I don't think I am ever like this.	Score 2
Sometimes	– I am sometimes like this.	Score 4
Average	– I am like this on average.	Score 6
Usually	– Most of the time I am like this.	Score 8
Always	– I think I am always like this.	Score 10

This will give an overall measure of your self-worth. Note this is not how you think other people see you, but how *you* see yourself.

Optimistic	4 X	Considerate	10
Tactful	4 X	Sensible	8
Responsible	8	Ambitious	10
Open-minded	8	Effective	4 X
Bright	10	Stable	4 Y
Confident	4 X	Honest	4 X
Aware	4 Y	Reasonable	6 X
Mature	10	Efficient	2 Y
Satisfied	2/4 X	Purposeful	4 X
Clear-thinking	6	Warm-hearted	6
Pleasant	4 X	Normal	10
Fair-minded	4 +	Understanding	6
Presentable	4 X	Total score part 1	148

Part 2

There is another measure: how you would *like* to see yourself. This time make the statement to yourself 'I would *like to be* an optimistic person', 'I would *like to be* a tactful person' and so on, then score Part 2 in the same way as in Part 1:

Never — I never want to be like this.   Score 2
Sometimes — I would sometimes like to be like this.   Score 4
Average — I'd like to be like this about half the time.   Score 6
Usually — I'd like to be like this most of the time.   Score 8
Always — I would like to be always like this.   Score 10

Optimistic	10 X	Considerate	8
Tactful	10 X	Sensible	8
Responsible	10 X	Ambitious	10 +
Open-minded	4	Effective	10 X
Bright	10 X	Stable	10 X
Confident	10 X	Honest	4
Aware	2/10	Reasonable	6
Mature	4	Efficient	10 X
Satisfied	8 +	Purposeful	10 X
Clear-thinking	4	Warm-hearted	10
Pleasant	10 X	Normal	10
Fair-minded	1	Understanding	10
Presentable	10 X	Total score part 2	199

Don't get in a twist about scores – whatever instinctively comes to mind is best for this purpose. Then add them up. Part 1 measures your overall self-image or self-worth.

◆ Over 200 indicates a very positive self-image.
◆ Between 150 and 200 suggests you have a generally positive self-image.
◆ Between 100 and 150 suggests your self-image is only partly positive.
◆ 50 to 100 suggests a generally negative self-image, although, as we saw earlier, it may be high in certain areas.

The Part 2 score measures how you would like to see yourself. Get the total, then take one score from the other to find the difference, or shortfall, between how you would like to be and how you think you are.

The difference in score also tells a story. This suggests how contented you are with yourself at present, and in what respects you would like to be different.

◆ 0 to 50 indicates you are contented with yourself.
◆ 50 to 100 suggests you are fairly contented with yourself.
◆ 100 to 150 suggests you are not really happy with yourself.
◆ More than 150 suggests you are very negative about yourself.

You should now know which areas you need to think about, and where to make changes. One or more of the low scores might account for a range of problems, such as procrastination, lack of achievement and pressure of time. Having identified these high difference scores also highlights the areas it is worth thinking about more, as you have already indicated that you would like to change. The low Part 1 scores, and the high Part 2 'differences' are the areas you should work on.

You may find that this self-image assessment fits with the quick self-rating you did in the last chapter, and what you wrote in your six-minute self-appraisal in Chapter 1. Alternatively there may be areas of self-belief of which you were not aware, but which could affect your behaviour and achievement. Identifying these factors, and a desire to change, are the biggest hurdles in solving any time problem. Tackling your top few disempowering beliefs is bound to bring big changes. Once you decide that a belief is outdated, illogical, or simply not useful, you are already on the way to discarding it. You are getting at the very heart of the matter, and change – change where it matters and where it has a long-term effect – is inevitable.

CHAPTER 5

Turning Dreams into Decisions

Y ou are unlikely to dream your way to success, or to accomplish some great feat, without doing something practical. Your behaviour, including your habits, must change. You have to want to do things – to be *motivated* to achieve your goals. Your values and beliefs must translate into actions that make the difference. Once you have strong, clear beliefs, and specific goals, you will do the things that will bring about your chosen outcomes. You will be a natural achiever – without much conscious thought. However, by understanding the process, and in particular the effect of unconscious drivers and motivators on your behaviour, you will be far more effective and have greater control.

This is one of the keys to productivity and time management. It is illustrated in the flush of output before leaving for holiday, or when we are driven by a reward that we value highly such as a certificate, cash bonus or recognition. In this chapter we will consider the main motivators, and how these relate to the values and beliefs we discussed in the earlier chapters.

Pleasure and pain

We have a natural tendency to move towards pleasure and away from pain, as we perceive them. So we tend to naturally do things we like doing, even if the pleasurable inputs are not producing outputs. But sometimes we will put up with pain – not necessarily physical pain, but anything we consider distasteful – in order to achieve a longer-term outcome we associate with pleasure. You will probably find that the goals that are high up on your hierarchy of goals, like financial independence or good health, mean pleasure to you. Lower down they will be a mixture of moving towards pleasure and away from pain (say by doing exercises to avoid poor health).

Both pleasure and pain are strong motivators, but in the long run the drive towards perceived pleasure seems to be stronger.

This tendency differs, however, from person to person. Some people are naturally positive, and seem always to be moving towards some pleasurable goal and enjoying life in the process. Others are more negative, and everything they do seems to be to avoid future pain. Perhaps they try to avoid being dependent in old age, illness, becoming lonely and so on.

> These pleasure/pain drivers are a deep part of our make-up. Just being aware of them can help us to understand and adjust our behaviour, including how we use our time.

The pleasure/pain principle is a useful one. It is often possible, for instance, to build pleasure into otherwise not-so-pleasant tasks, as a driver or motivator. After all, it is only how we *perceive* things that creates 'pleasure' or 'pain'.

Universal needs

We all have basic needs. Psychologists have tried to identify these and have come up with similar short-lists of what drives us to do things. A simple model, for example, suggests four basic psychological needs:

◆ The need to live.
◆ The need to love and be loved.
◆ The need to feel important.
◆ The need to experience variety.

The 'need to live' includes basic elements like air, food, water and shelter. It is an incredibly strong instinct and people will go to amazing lengths when they think their physical survival is in jeopardy. The desire for security of different kinds, good health, and safety, which you might consider longer-term life goals, all stem from this basic survival need.

The need for love shows up in goals to do with relationships. It can be almost as powerful as the basic need to survive.

The need to feel important is to do with recognition and personal identity. Children display this need very openly – 'Look what I've done mum.' Adults tend to suppress it, but it crops up all the time, sometimes in the way we try to take credit for what others have done, and the many behaviours that are concerned with getting noticed.

The need for variety is also expressed in different ways, such as the different types of food we eat, clothes we wear, or books we read. Without a variety of sensations around us we quickly vegetate as human beings. In the extreme, people will try all sorts of things, even putting themselves at risk, in an attempt to bring newness and variety into their lives.

The source of motivation

These basic needs can work together, but sometimes they are in conflict. If a person has a powerful need to feel important, for instance, they may be prepared to go to any length, sometimes forgoing other needs such as being loved, in the process. At any time all four basic needs are being met to some degree. However, one need might be stronger than the others, although this can change as we grow older and go through different life experiences.

These needs are the source of all motivation. It is where behaviour is 'born'. Regardless of whether a person is goal-oriented, ambitious, or a 'stick in the mud', each of these basic needs will manifest itself in one way or another. Being able to identify how these needs express themselves is an important part of knowing yourself. It helps align your beliefs and goals, and is part of the key time management process of setting priorities.

Motivation is one of the biggest factors in managing time, and it helps to know how you are motivated as a person. Try to answer the following questions. What motivates me to:

- ◆ Get out of bed in the morning?
- ◆ Start a new task?
- ◆ Complete a job I have got bored with?
- ◆ Be polite to people?
- ◆ Work harder?
- ◆ Plan more?
- ◆ Achieve deadlines?
- ◆ Want to do better next time?
- ◆ Learn new things?

Your answers to these questions will give valuable clues about
how your behaviour, and probably the way you think, need to
change. If you think of enough examples you will also probably
find that your behaviour follows broad 'strategies' of attitude
and behaviour. The following exercise allows you to identify
some of these, with a view to trying other strategies to see if
they work better. It is unlikely that your answer will be a
definite either/or, so put a mark somewhere along a continuum
based on your instinctive answer.

Try it now   An exercise to identify personal patterns of motivation.

I tend to be motivated:

By people   By things
|_____|

By outside factors   By internal criteria
|_____|

Towards pleasure   Away from pain
|_____|

By fear of failure   By anticipating success
|_____|

To start things   To finish things
|_____|

The previous exercise reflects the way we think and the patterns
of thought structures which have become familiar and
comfortable – whether effective or not. Like any other
thoughts, these can be reprogrammed so that we are better
motivated and achieve more.

The map is not the territory

Our basic needs result in wide variations in behaviour. They
reflect both common tendencies such as those in the above
exercise, and also countless personal 'strategies' special to us.
For example, we may envisage an outcome in vivid pictures, or
be warned against doing something by an 'inner voice', or
simply have a 'feeling' that we want to get on and do
something. We are also influenced by what we believe, our
values, and any rules we might apply to our behaviour. So a

simple universal needs model is of little practical use on its own. It has to be linked particularly with the self-beliefs we have already discussed.

It is as if we each see our world through a unique window, or in accordance with our own perceptual 'map' of reality. Each of our maps is different, because of our background and the unique set of life experiences that have brought us to where we are today. None of our individual maps represents reality, but is a filtered version of what is really happening outside. We see, for instance, *what our brain sees* rather than what passes through the optic process. Beliefs also share this efficient processing system, although they do not always serve us well.

Relating self-beliefs to basic needs

We said earlier that our higher-level beliefs are supported by more specific ones, to form – just like our goals – a hierarchy. Our basic needs are also part of this hierarchy, and each belief will in turn relate to one or more fundamental life need. The belief 'bald tyres are dangerous' relates, for instance, to the need to live, and to avoid life-threatening situations. The belief 'top management are only interested in themselves' probably stems from the need to feel important. The belief 'I'm in good health for my age' might support all basic needs: feeling important because you do better than your contemporaries in terms of health and fitness; drawing on the love and relationship benefits that you might associate with keeping healthy and no doubt looking younger; perhaps enjoying a variety of social life through your health activities; trying new programmes and diets; and no doubt an awareness of the link with longer life and survival.

These fundamental needs are transformed into hundreds of beliefs, about ourselves, other people, and the world around, that form the basis of all our behaviour. Our core values also reflect these basic needs (see Figure 7).

Relating beliefs to life-rules

There is another element in this model before beliefs are translated into behaviour. We each have rules that govern most

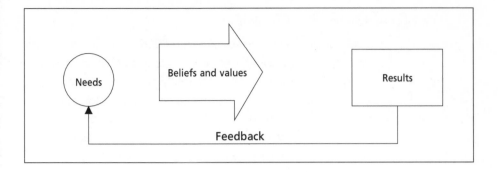

Fig. 7. Needs into beliefs and values.

of what we do. Each rule can account for many individual behaviours, and the rules themselves are simply the outworking of our beliefs. So, for example, the belief 'Top management are only interested in themselves' might result in rules such as 'Always cover yourself for any decisions you make', 'Don't rely on job security', or 'Join a union.' These rules are formed, in effect, by asking 'if . . .what then?' If 'I'm no good in front of a large group' (the belief) then 'Avoid getting into situations where that might happen', 'Keep a low profile', 'Always have excuses lined up', 'Don't try for a manager's position', 'Don't win the top sales award', and so on (the rules). These rules immediately translate into behaviour. They sometimes explain behaviour that is apparently irrational, anti-social, or stupid. As with higher-level beliefs, we rarely stop to think about these rules which unconsciously guide all our behaviour.

Try it now	Compile a personal list of such rules for different areas of your life, such as work, family, hobbies and so on. Then see if you can relate each rule, first to a *belief* – which you may have already identified – then to a *basic life need*. You are then free to question whether a rule is useful or valid, and whether you want to discard it. You are also free to question the belief upon which it is based. Having identified the need such a rule supports, you might well think of other, better ways to fulfil the need.

This exercise will open up more acceptable, easier, or quicker choices, and disturb some comfortable mental patterns which may not be serving you well at present.

Dynamic model of motivation

These needs, values, beliefs and rules motivate us to the actions that bring about results – there is always some behaviour, and always some outcome. An inner feedback system then checks whether the behaviour meets our basic needs, conforms to our beliefs, and is likely to achieve our hoped-for outcomes.

The process is a dynamic one. We frequently change what we do in an attempt to get a better, more successful outcome, but usually sticking to our own 'rules'. Sometimes we change a rule, however, if it has been overtaken by experience or new knowledge. For example, you might get to know one of your top managers personally and change your belief about top management, and the rules that you follow as a consequence. Or you might visit a sausage factory and change your rules about what food you eat.

However, change is the exception rather than the rule, especially at the higher belief levels, and certainly as regards our main, core values. We need to *intervene* in some way to change some beliefs – do something – so that they are in line with what we now want. Changing behaviour means bringing the whole brain into play. This especially includes the visualising right brain that can 'see' us in the way we want to see ourselves. Our basic needs, of course, never change, although their relative weighting might. We will always ensure that somehow they are met.

The whole process, including the feedback, can be represented by the model shown in Figure 8.

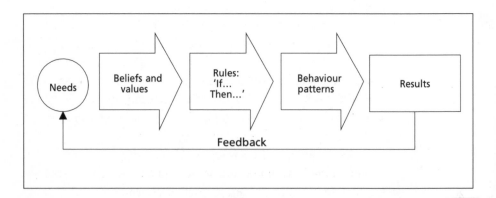

Fig. 8. Needs into results.

This model helps us to understand how we are motivated to do what we do. That's what managing time is all about. It doesn't mean that we have to consciously question everything we do and analyse every action. On the contrary, we are at our best when we are 'unconsciously competent'. That means our skills are so automatic that we can excel in the tasks we are doing 'without thinking', and so give more focused, conscious attention to what we deem important. But at the same time, beliefs will not change of their own accord. Left alone, they may actually be reinforced in a self-fulfilling spiral – negative or positive, disempowering or empowering. We leave positive self-beliefs well alone. With negative beliefs, we have to intervene in the process.

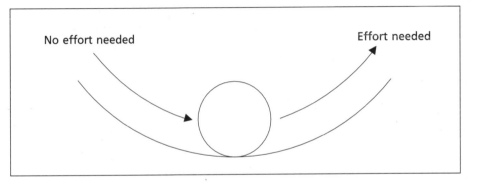

Fig. 9. The comfort zone.

At the minimum, solving the time problem will mean getting out of your comfort zone (Figure 9), and a bit of mental reprogramming. But with each change you will take greater control over your time and life.

Hang-ups

We sometimes describe the negative beliefs through which our experience is filtered as hang-ups. They result from real or imagined previous experiences that have given us a jaundiced approach to a particular situation. They are effective blocks on our flow of energy, interest and motivation. It is normal to recall earlier experiences whenever we meet a new situation, and to call upon comfortable, supportive beliefs. This is a useful survival mechanism – seeking to match new situations with familiar ones – but feedback that hampers achieving our present goals is of little use. Negative memories and self-beliefs, or hang-ups, have to be recognised for what they are. We can then make the conscious decision to discard them as operating strategies.

A common hang-up relates to making speeches, and public speaking ranks as one of the top phobias. There is often no rational basis for such a negative self-belief. Some event, no doubt, starts off the downward spiral. For example, in Susan's case she rewrites her speech several times, putting in lots of time and effort, staying up late the night before to practise it. She is not sure what to wear, and fusses over small details. She worries herself sick about blowing it, or freezing in the middle of the speech. She gets little sleep. By the time she gets to the meeting she is tired and tense, oblivious to what the previous speakers say, so misses important points she could have brought into her speech. She gets into a cold sweat and drops her papers going up to the rostrum. Then it is downhill. She mumbles her introduction and hardly looks at the audience. Nobody is impressed, some are embarrassed, some are asleep and some are annoyed.

Note that the hang-up is more powerful than the hard effort and long hours of practice she put in. It's not for want of willpower and trying. This is a prime way to misuse time, spending it – lots of it – on efforts that do not bring about the results we are after.

Choosing change

These sorts of feelings are all too common and govern most of our waking lives. Lack of output or shortage of time usually have their origin not in lack of intelligence, skill or even willpower, but in a variety of feelings, beliefs and attitudes that operate a bit too far below the surface to be spotted and dealt with. Such situations are ripe for right-brain visualisation methods. It is important to plan for a speech, of course, but Susan did plenty of that. Perhaps specific coaching could have given her the added skills she needed, and also the confidence that comes from practising in front of others. But the important factor is self-image. That's what fuels confidence and more or less determines behaviour.

> We act out what we think we are, and we have got to have a 'mental script' to work to.

Susan's mental rehearsal should concentrate, therefore, not so much on the detail of the speech, but on seeing herself as an accomplished speechmaker. She should concentrate on *being* as well as doing, realistically and repeatedly embracing the feared experience.

Leftovers from childhood

Until you are ready to make changes, learn to accept your hang-ups. They are simply leftovers of valid childhood survival tactics. They have served you well. You may have been ridiculed as a child, for instance, found it unpleasant, and decided to avoid situations that might bring pain. Maybe your logic was wrong, and you made 2+2=5. But your intention was sensible from where you then were, in your limited childhood world.

> We are no longer children. We can make decisions. We can learn and acquire new skills.

Sadly, we don't adjust our 'thinking strategies' to reflect all the changes around us.

Try it now   List any beliefs about yourself that may form hang-ups. You may have already identified some when doing the life-rules exercise earlier. Then, in conjunction with your hierarchy of goals, decide which beliefs are useful for your present outcomes (empowering, on balance) and those that are likely to be disempowering. Finally, give yourself a few good reasons why you should discard certain hang-ups, and decide to do so.

Who is in charge?

Who makes the pleasure or pain decisions? How are we driven or drawn towards our outcomes? The hang-ups that affect our behaviour are very much part of us, and the more we think about our goals and self-beliefs, the more we identify different aspects of our personality. The assertive self might be operating at one moment, and then the tactful self takes over. We each have a complex make-up. The distinction between the logical left brain and the holistic right brain is only one, albeit a fundamental aspect of these different selves.

Transactional analysis, which considers the parent, adult and child in each of us, is another way these selves are in evidence. Sometimes the highly organised, time efficient self runs your day, and another time the indecisive 'you' wins over, and you (the one who should be in charge) accomplish nothing. These vagaries of feelings and attitudes are often blamed on people and circumstances. In fact such moods and mental strategies are long-standing parts of our make-up.

The 'you' at home may be different from the 'you' at work. And that is a clue for self-management. You can call upon known parts of yourself. Sometimes a bit of switching can work wonders. For instance, you can make use of the creativity you display in a hobby or some personal interest at work, or the discipline and professionalism of your work in a domestic or social situation. You may behave differently in different surroundings, in which case you can make changes to your environment to create a certain stimulus. Inner resources are always there, somewhere.

> Awareness of these many parts of us, and the techniques for creating and changing mental strategies, can make allies of these inner critics. You are then in charge.

The power of decisions

Top time managers know when to make up their minds. This is often hard to do, and one reason why many people avoid too much introspection is that they know they will have to face personal choices and tricky decisions. But most of us know that once we have made a firm decision, even if what we have to do is hard or distasteful, it becomes much easier from then on. The real turning point is in our attitude, what we believe about something, and the decision.

Whatever you are today – the job you are in, the interests and hobbies you pursue, where you live – involved decisions. Some were minor ones, but even these might have had a ripple, or cumulative effect on your life. Others were clearly turning points affecting the rest of your life. The future will be no different. It will be determined by the decisions you make about your goals, which we covered in Chapter 3, and how you will achieve them. But the *outcome decisions* are the most important – the 'what' rather than the 'how', what you want to do and be rather than the many actions you will need to fulfil your goal. As you think about what you want, be ready to make some decisions. Get into the habit of writing your goals down, so you can refer back to them and get encouragement for having been positive and goal-oriented.

That's what personal success is all about, and the foundation of getting the best out of your time.

> Even deciding to make one important decision can be life changing.

Real time management does not just tinker at the edges, it requires courageous decisions.

Decisions of heart or mind

Making decisions is usually associated with high-level, logical thinking, but the reality is different. All our attitudes, self-beliefs and feelings come into play in the decisions we make. Many of our decisions today relate as much to the values and perceptions we acquired in childhood as to the 'facts' or 'logic' of particular situations.

As children our decisions are normally made for us, and this conditioning is very powerful, reinforced by the authority figures that remain throughout later life. In fact, many people never take full control of their own lives. They assume that they have few real choices and expect the boss, the government, their spouse, or some other authority figure to make the important decisions for them, put things right when they go wrong, and give them what they want. Others accept their parents' authority less completely, yet still in effect imitate them to gain the power and authority they seemed to have. Conversely, a more rebellious child might in later life do the opposite of what their parents would have done, even if it does not make them happy.

None of this is likely to be rational, and it invariably goes on below our consciousness. Most intelligent adults will deny that they are influenced in any way in the decisions they make. But once you are aware of the factors, and the beliefs themselves that you have already identified, you can start to make better choices.

Living with past decisions

Think back over the major experiences and events in your life, good and bad, and list them. Add your approximate age, and whether what happened, as you look back, was good or bad. For example, you might list:

◆ went to college, 18, good
◆ fell in deep end at baths, 4, bad
◆ passed driving test, 18, good
◆ got Nottingham post, 30, bad

and so on. Go back as far as you can remember.

Rearrange these in chronological order. Then, beginning at the bottom of your list, ask yourself these questions and answer them thoughtfully:

◆ Did I have a choice about what happened? Answer yes or no.
◆ What kind of decision did I make as a result of what happened?
◆ How did it affect my beliefs and attitudes?
◆ Have I learned from this experience?

You may find that you continue to interpret experiences, or the decisions you make following an experience, in the way you did as a child. For instance you might say to yourself:

◆ I will get my own back on him.
◆ I will never speak in front of a large group again.
◆ I will never go camping.
◆ I will not trust insurance agents.
◆ I will not let anyone know I have failed.
◆ I will not say 'no'.

Such decisions are as likely to be based on the hang-ups of early conditioning as on a rational, common sense response to the experience. Hopefully, there will be an abrupt change from teenage onwards as to whether you consider you had a choice, reflecting a more adult way of thinking and responsibility for your own outcomes. But for many people the feeling of dependence continues, and long-standing beliefs dictate their behaviour and decisions. These mental patterns, or 'strategies', once recognised, are immediately open to change, and this is where the big improvements in time management are to be made.

The bottom line is that you can make whatever decisions you like – even decisions about your values and self-beliefs. Being willing to make courageous decisions, firmly and frequently, is a feature of good time managers.

CHAPTER 6

Taking Control of Your Feelings

M otivation is about how you feel. And how you feel about something affects your behaviour – whether you do something or don't do something, whether you complete a task in half an hour or two or three hours, or even whether you finish a task at all. Often the causes of our day-to-day fluctuations in feelings are not identified. We just 'don't feel on form'. These feelings, of course, can quickly change. You may, for instance, immerse yourself in activity, concentrating more fully on the job in hand. Sometimes we consciously psych ourselves out of a feeling, and at other times events just overtake them unconsciously.

Changing the shape of thoughts

How we think (and feel) is represented by the way we perceive things inwardly. This is largely an unconscious process, associated with right-brain processing. In situations when you feel positive and enthusiastic, your thought representation is likely to be clear and focused visually, with strong inner senses generally – including hearing and feeling. A strongly visualised anticipated future outcome – a promotion, holiday, or new car, for instance – gets close to the 'reality' that you experience through your external senses. The quality of this reality is reflected in the so-called 'submodalities', or characteristics of our inner seeing, hearing and feeling 'modalities' (see Figure 10).

These submodalities together determine how we 'feel' about something. For example, different happy memories, whilst no doubt having very different content, may tend to adopt the same pattern of submodalities in each of the these main representation systems. Less pleasant, or disempowering thoughts on the other hand, will adopt different characteristics, again regardless of their content.

Visual	
Brightness	Contrast
Size	Clarity
Colour/black and white	Focus
Saturation (vividness)	Framed/panoramic
Hue or colour balance	Movement
Shape	Perspective
Location	Associated/dissociated
Distance	Three-dimensional/flat
Auditory	
Pitch	Duration
Tempo (speed)	Location
Volume	Distance
Rhythm	External/internal
Continuous/interrupted	Source
Timbre or tonality	Mono/stereo
Digital (words)	Clarity
Associated/dissociated	Number
Kinaesthetic (sensations)	
Pressure	Movement
Location	Duration
Number	Intensity
Texture	Shape
Temperature	Frequency (tempo)

Fig. 10. Modalities and submodalities.

As conscious human beings we have the ability to change these thought submodalities, and thus affect how we feel, and in consequence how we behave and what we achieve.

Try it now   This is an exercise in changing how you feel. Recollect any specific memorable event in your life and 'replay' it as vividly as you can – first the sights, then sounds, then feelings. Run through the memory as if you were experiencing it all over again. You will find that your present feelings match how you felt at the time recalled. Indeed, your physiology – your body posture, breathing and facial expression etc – will match your new state. More importantly, you can *change* the various characteristics, or submodalities, and thus change how you feel about the memory, regardless of its content.

In the case of an unpleasant memory, for instance, try making the pictures big, bright and panoramic, seeing things through your own eyes ('associated') rather than looking at yourself as through the eyes of a third party ('dissociated'). You can then change any voices and other sounds, making them more pleasant, or even comical. A man's voice can instantly be switched to a little girl's, for instance. Try it. Anything is possible in the imagination. In the same way you can manipulate senses of touch and other feelings the memory induces.

Switching submodalities

When these submodality switches are carried out deliberately and repeatedly, they will affect your fundamental attitudes and beliefs in relation to the memory. This is the basis of techniques that have been used to cure all sorts of phobias. In the same way, a future task, which is anticipated as being unpleasant or painful, can be reprogrammed.

Try it now

Here's how you switch submodalities. Simply identify the various submodalities present in tasks you enjoy doing. Imagine yourself doing the task, carefully noting the different characteristics in each of the three main representation systems. Then apply these to your visualisation of the unpleasant task, by exchanging the submodalities of your anticipated experience with the positive, pleasant ones you have identified. This will change how you feel about the upcoming event or situation. Applying the technique seriously, the change will be permanent.

You can reinforce these changes by various anchoring techniques that ensure the brain instantly associates with the empowering memory you desire (see Further Reading).

Mental rehearsal

Not only is your attitude to a problem or task (which no doubt is a time robber) changed by mental imagery, but also repeated visualisation acts as a sort of mental rehearsal. It's like having extra practice, so you become both skilled and confident in the imagined behaviours. Entertainers and sportspeople are familiar with such skills, and some use them to great effect.

These techniques involve right-brain imagery, and can be used to change any of the negative self-beliefs you identified earlier. Simply swap the empowering submodalities from a behaviour reflecting a positive self-image into a visualised behaviour reflecting a negative self-belief.

Motivational pull

These visualisation techniques have an important effect, which increases your motivation. By making a future, longer-term goal more real, you increase its motivational 'pull'. Let's say you are working towards a part-time degree. The final reward seems a long time in the future, and does not keep you sufficiently motivated. By clearly and repeatedly visualising the benefits of your outcome, your mind can bridge the intervening time gap, and so create its own inner motivation. Young athletes, visualising their dream of a medal or some other accolade of success, can remain motivated year after year against all the odds. Entrepreneurs can stay highly motivated with the dream of success.

Giving yourself rewards

Sometimes the perceived benefits that will accrue from spending your time in a certain way are not enough to motivate you. In that case you are free to decide on your own external motivators. You can create a short-term return on the investment of your time. Different things motivate people in different ways, of course. Sometimes the welcome thought of a cup of coffee can keep you going for a while longer, or maybe the treat of a walk in the park, or switching to a job you really enjoy doing. Bigger rewards like having a meal out that evening or allowing yourself to indulge in spending on yourself can also help. The attractiveness of the reward will affect the degree of motivation. This does not mean that a reward needs to have real money value.

Perceiving pain and pleasure

As we saw, it is the perception of pain or pleasure that makes the difference. As a child, leaving certain types of food you like to the end of the meal, for example, is reward enough to get you through the items you are not too keen on. The principle holds good. A genuine, real break of a few minutes can act as an incentive. Although costing you time, it will be well repaid in outputs.

The important thing is that we all respond to rewards, internally and externally. This is part of our desire for pleasure rather than pain. You can build rewards into your life to ensure ongoing motivation and the best use of time. It starts with the goal-setting you met in Chapter 3.

The time management secret is to get to know yourself enough to be able to apply rewards in different situations so that you get more and more control over your feelings, and how you spend your time. Your objective should be to do with your time what is best to achieve your various outcomes, even though in some cases you may have to endure perceived pain to bring about an important outcome.

Special treats

How can you exploit this reward principle? If you like putting your feet up and reading a favourite magazine, don't indulge in this except in return for carrying out a task you know has to be done. For a major task, it usually pays well to decide on a special treat. But do this up front, rather than deciding on it when you have completed the task. It will then act as a motivator both to get you started and to keep you going all the way through. Like a forthcoming holiday, your imagined pleasure can see you through months of less motivating times. The chances are, the reward motivator will mean you complete the task more quickly than you would otherwise have done, so it is a positive time management device. You will have to use your visualising right brain, first to creatively think up rewards, and then to fix the clear mental picture to which you are motivated.

Mini-rewards

Long jobs may have to be broken down into smaller chunks, and you may also have to decide on mini-rewards to keep you motivated. Sometimes the intrinsic pleasure of doing a job well is sufficient reward. This is why setting realistic, motivating goals in the first place is so important. But on other occasions you will have to plan a few 'pats on the back'. Time itself can be a reward – time to yourself, to do whatever you like. This can be a wise investment, as the extra motivation it gives will save much more time than it costs you. Time to yourself will no doubt also achieve other less tangible outcomes, perhaps to do with your own self-development, health and happiness. In other words, it is a legitimate input, because it supports one of your goals, even if not the task in hand (check back on the hierarchy of goals in Chapter 3). Time to yourself can be planned into your life along with the other goals. The reward effect is also still achieved, as we saw earlier (leaving your favourite food to the end), by changing the order of what you do to maintain maximum motivation.

Positive stress and flow states

We each have different resources that we bring to a job, and we also have different thresholds of stress. Some people thrive on big challenges, whilst others 'blank out' quickly. Most of us know the feeling of being so swamped with work, either in quantity or complexity, that we go into a tailspin, effectively doing nothing towards meeting the challenge. We might appear to be busy and active (that's a popular, well-honed skill), but we are mentally closing our eyes to reality. We can't face up to the real task – the outcome as we discussed in Chapter 3. We also know what it is to be bored with a job, or to cringe at the very thought of starting something. Jobs in either category are likely to result in lots of unproductive time. We cannot bring ourselves to give of our best.

Try it now   This exercise is about identifying non-motivators. Identify tasks that you find easy, take in your stride, or treat as routine. Note those that you find boring, and for which you cannot get motivated. Then identify jobs that have caused you anxiety because they were beyond your ability or resources, were just too big, or for which you were given an unreasonable deadline. Notice the effect that either kind of job has on your motivation.

From what you have learned so far about motivation and setting goals, think about what you can do to reduce the boredom of easy jobs and the stress of more difficult ones so that you work at maximum motivation and peak performance. Consider, for example:

◆ the size of the task
◆ how you picture the goal you are aiming for
◆ your resources and skill in relation to the task
◆ what would make the task exciting and challenging
◆ your beliefs about your ability in the particular activity in question.

Healthy stress and flow

Somewhere in between there is an optimal level of healthy stress, which produces optimal performance. This level of stress differs from person to person. You may find that simply by increasing the challenge of a job you automatically do it better and quicker, as all your body and mind resources are brought into play. This is another smart and enjoyable way to improve your time management.

When we are working at the right level of stress we can accomplish far more in a given time. Most of us are familiar with a state of 'flow' in which everything seems to come right and we can get through copious amounts of work without difficulty. There is pleasure in even the most demanding tasks when we feel that we are giving everything, and we get the results. This state of mastery is related to how we rate the task as compared with how we rate our own ability to perform it, as illustrated in Figure 11.

Often by stretching ourselves beyond what we have mastered in the past, we call on extra resources and move up to another dimension of achievement. This special state is associated with a rush of adrenaline and not a little nervousness, but also with the thrill of self-development, achievement, creativity and new learning.

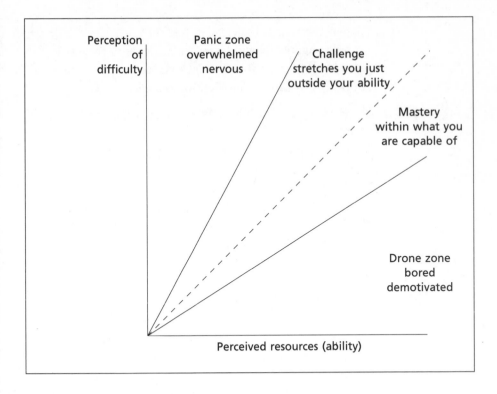

Fig. 11. Flow states.

Try it now   You can learn to harness your peak performance strategy. Think about tasks you have done at peak performance level, when you felt stretched and highly motivated. Consider what might be recurring features so that you can change how you think and what you do in the future. For example:

- ◆ the length of the job
- ◆ the technical complexity
- ◆ the person you work with or for
- ◆ your experience and training
- ◆ the kind of task (working with numbers, the level of detail, working with computers, etc).

Then ask:

- ◆ 'Is there anything you can do that will increase your perception of
  (a) the job, and/or
- ◆ (b) your ability to do it

that will increase its challenge to you?'

Your objective should be to make as many activities as possible fall into the zone in which you are motivated to work at peak performance. Consider, for example:

◆ changing the tasks themselves (say by making them bigger or smaller)
◆ improving your actual ability (say by better planning or skill training)
◆ changing how you think about tasks (perhaps questioning the self-beliefs on which your perceptions are based)
◆ fitting jobs into a bigger context both of other personal goals, and also of your organisation.

The peak performance balance

The balance of a peak performance state is a fine one, and the phenomenon is all to do with perceptions. On the one hand we have a perception of the level of difficulty of a task, and on the other hand we have some perception of our own resources, or ability to achieve the task. If the job seems too difficult, and we do not think we have the ability, we can get into a state of nervousness or panic. On the other hand, if we are confident in our ability and the job seems too easy, we can become bored and demotivated. Either way we will not work effectively, and will make very bad use of our time.

Our threshold of stress and the relationship between the task and our resources changes, of course, as any relationship is dynamic. Success breeds success, and as we become more and more confident of our ability we need tasks that are more demanding, to operate at a new level of mastery or challenge.

CHAPTER 7

Thinking and Planning

A popular way to think about how we use our time is the idea of investing it, as we would our money, in the hope of a good return – a payback – some time in the future. This supports the idea of valuing time as a scarce resource, and the need to decide on our priorities and values. It also links closely with *opportunity cost* that we met earlier, a term that also crops up when considering where to get the best value from any investment. This chapter considers time management from the point of view of the payback it gives, but applying some right-brain perspectives.

Payback time

There is a lot of sense in the payback approach. The time you might spend on tidying your desk or rearranging the filing system is unlikely to fulfil any immediate outcome on your list of goals such as sales, reduced costs, bottom line profits – or health. But looked on as a *time investment*, the picture becomes very different. If a tidy desk enables you to work more efficiently in doing other tasks that directly contribute to your effectiveness (like responding promptly to correspondence that might bring about real business outcomes) the time you spend tidying your desk – apparently unproductively – might pay big dividends. This is even more so in the case of a bigger time investment in the filing system, with an even greater, although maybe longer-term, potential payback.

Investing for the long-term or short-term

Some activities only make sense when viewed over a long timescale. In the case of rearranging the filing system you might lose out in the short-term because you are unfamiliar with the new system and it takes you longer to locate files. But the new arrangement is no doubt aimed at giving bigger benefits in the longer term. These benefits are likely to be both positive (say quicker access, or better cross-referring) and negative (avoiding an overload with a rush of activity).

The positive and negative implications involved in any 'time spent' decision relate, of course, to the universal pain and pleasure drivers we have already met. We seek either to increase pleasure – the better life the tidy desk or all-singing-dancing filing system offers – or to avoid the pain of what might happen if we don't invest the time. More commonly, both forces are at work at the same time.

> The payback or investment factor is always present in how we spend our time, even if we do not consciously consider it.

Valuing future outcomes today

Outcomes are central to the way we best use time, and whatever we do depends upon how we value those outcomes. But the timing of outcomes – how far into the future they will happen – is also a big factor. We value an outcome very differently depending on when it is likely to occur – by tonight, the end of the year, or upon reaching retirement age, for example. The amount of time we will spend to achieve the outcome (the input) will have a value, and that must relate in turn to the outcome we are working towards, and how badly we want it. It doesn't make sense to exert great effort for an outcome we do not value. But what of a valued outcome that will happen a long time in the future?

The present value of an outcome

Accountants use the idea of the present value of money when appraising an investment that involves receiving (or saving) money or paying it out in the future, upon which is based the technique of *discounted cash flow*. DCF methods recognise that the value of money is reduced the further in the future you are to receive it. The idea fits neatly with far older wisdom like 'A bird in the hand is worth two in the bush.'

When we use our time (say studying late each night for a degree in three years' time), we are investing in the hope of future benefits. However, we instinctively value outcomes a long time in the future lower than those that are more immediate. So, for example, we might readily spend an hour tidying our desk to ensure we get off a couple of hours early at the end of the week for the start of our holiday, but not, perhaps, for the far bigger but long-term benefits that might result. If our hard work on the desk precedes a visit from the regional boss and our half-yearly appraisal, and salary review, that very afternoon, our motivation and time investment will be so much greater.

In the case of studying for a degree, we might go crazy with last-minute swotting when the prize of the degree is so near and so highly valued. In every case, the value of the outcome, coupled with the timing of the possible benefit, will affect the time, energy and ingenuity we are likely to put into it.

This helps to explain the pre-holiday miracles we all achieve – the outcome is both high value and immediate. It also explains why we tend to put off even the most important jobs that will only give benefit in the long-term. The further we look into the future, the less certain things are anyway – whether good or bad outcomes. And the unconscious mind seems to discount this uncertainty by lowering the pleasure or pain of a future experience. This is a natural tendency. Whether or not we do the 'sums', we unconsciously apply the principles.

The hierarchy of outcome value

If you look back at your hierarchy of goals, you will notice that the higher up the hierarchy, the more important are the outcomes. Towards the top they represent your 'life goals'. You will also notice that these goals – such as security, happiness, or contentment – tend to be longer term. Their benefits (more pleasure and less pain) are perceived as happening well into the future.

> We have a hierarchy of values, or importance, which discounts each outcome based on when it will happen, and the perceived benefit or pleasure it gives.

So, for example, winning the league this season might rank higher than saving for a retirement home, or getting promotion next month might rank higher than losing half a stone in weight by Christmas. Like any other human tendency or habit, this short-termism, once recognised, can be changed, or even harnessed to serve you better.

Holistic logic

All this means that we don't always do what left-brain 'logic' might tell us to do. That's because we don't just think in a logical way. Sometimes, however, our instinctive decisions turn out to be the best. We know from experience, for example, that the longer in the future an outcome is (like receiving settlement of a debt) the more likelihood there is that things can go wrong, so the lower the chance of achieving the outcome. This instinctively *feels* right, so our behaviour reflects it. We tend to go for ready cash, for example, rather than post-dated cheques of higher value.

> The instinctive, even unconscious, process in which we not only rank our outcomes by value, but we 'discount' their value to take account of time, has a holistic logic of its own.

In turn, we adjust the time and effort we are prepared to invest in those outcomes (the inputs) accordingly. And all this – the values, the priorities, the beliefs and rules that support everything we do with our time – usually happens without thinking in any conscious sense. This is the intuitive approach, and illustrates the sophistication of right-brain thinking applied to time management. By understanding and harnessing the process, you can start to adjust your behaviour in a way that capitalises on natural 'cybernetic', goal-seeking tendencies and maximises performance.

Tapping into your natural goal-achieving system

You can decide on which outcomes are most important, however far into the future they are. You can work the system. Here's what you can do, for instance, without resorting to technical systems or outside techniques.

♦ Enhance the motivating effect of a distant outcome by clear visualisation, concentrating on each modality (seeing, hearing, feeling) separately before bringing them together as a realistic mental rehearsal of the outcome.

♦ Decide upon some evidence and tangible benefits of achieving your outcome, and incorporate these into your visualisation.

♦ 'Chunk down' your outcomes into smaller ones, thus making each phase or part of the outcome happen sooner. Remember, however, the optimal size of the task to be stretched and challenged to achieve your best.

♦ Introduce rewards to add to your motivation, including simply changing the order of your tasks.

♦ Invest a bit of time thinking through your task, and any problems you are likely to encounter. When you feel you are getting nowhere or are bogged down, forget about it! Incubate the matter- sleep on it, and get on with something else.

♦ Be ready with a notepad in case ideas come to you when you least expect it.

♦ Keep referring to your hierarchy of goals, so that you know clearly where you are going, even if several intervening outcomes remain to be achieved.

♦ Use imagination rather than logic to get fired up.

An early payback

As well as wanting to maximise our time investment we usually want an early payback. The idea of payback is used universally in capital investments. You spend £100,000, say, and get your money back through the cash you generate in three years. Your payback is three years. On the face of it, you go for this investment rather than one that gives you your money back in five years. That makes sense, until you consider the longer term. Over a ten-year period, for example, the five-year payback might yield a far higher overall return. More often than not, however, a fast payback wins the day, regardless of the longer-term irrationality.

The same irrationality is displayed in the way we evaluate time investments. With the passage of time comes uncertainty and doubt. Ultimately, at a personal level, the question 'Will I be around to enjoy these benefits?' is bound to arise – and that surely makes sense. We can't live out our life entirely for some future benefit we may never enjoy. So short-termism rules. And it sometimes takes a whack on the head, and a careful appraisal of our many outcomes – big and small, work and personal, short-term and long-term – to make any sense of it all.

Time spent today is in the nature of an investment. It can produce benefits out of all proportion to the time input. But, in the nature of any investment, some of the benefits will be long-term, and in the nature of human outcomes many will be hard to quantify in a way that fits orthodox time management techniques. So the urgent/important decision requires more than ABC ranking systems. You need intuition and wisdom. A decision will hinge on how you value the big, intangible goals.

Payback questions

Here are some questions to ask yourself:

◆ What payback will I get from this activity/time spent? What outputs will I actually experience, and how will these contribute to my higher goals?

◆ When will the output occur? What interim benefits can I expect? What longer term benefits can I identify? Are there spin-off benefits in the longer term?

◆ Can I make the payback sooner? Can I make it bigger – get more for my time and effort? Or both?

◆ If I had to double my payback, what might I do differently, or omit?

◆ If I had to halve the time I spend to achieve the same output, what would I do differently?

◆ Are there other paybacks I have not identified? What are the indirect benefits of doing a task I have been putting off for a long time?

◆ What can I give myself as a reward for doing a distasteful or difficult task? What rewards would make me finish the job more quickly?

◆ What changes would I need to make to a task so that I do not need any reward – such that the reward is just in the doing?

◆ How does a person who enjoys doing what I dislike see things differently? How do they motivate themselves? What is their attitude to that sort of work, or a specific task?

◆ Is there something else I could be spending my time on that would give me a bigger and/or earlier payback?

◆ Can I enjoy my payback 'in advance' by clearly visualising it – just like a forthcoming holiday? Or part of it – just like a downpayment?

◆ What can I spend my time on that gives both work and leisure payback – that benefits me overall?

◆ In what different context might I feel better about the job I have to do?

◆ What might I spend my time on that would give a very high payback, in the form of saving me lots of time in the future?

◆ For me what payback, or outcome, would take precedence over everything else? 'If only I could have/do/be that . . .' What smaller outcomes might help bring this about? What would be the big changes to the way I use my time?

The answers to these questions will not come through a sophisticated time recording and analysis system. You will have to call on your innate creativity – which is exactly what we all do on the occasions we surprise ourselves and excel in what we are doing. With the right positive attitude we can all convert natural thinking processes into big improvements in performance.

> Think payback – not in an economic sense, but in the sense of getting more of whatever you want in whatever limited time you have.

The 'time problem' – if there was one – then solves itself.

Investing yourself

The more we think about time, the more unique a resource we see it to be. Time is not just something you 'get' or 'have', and it cannot be borrowed from someone who seems to have too much. When you spend time, you spend a bit of your life. And how you spend your time, probably more than anything else, defines the sort of person you are – your values, beliefs, your goals, and your unique personality. So investing your time is like investing yourself, with all that entails.

Saving or spending?

How you use your time not only determines the sort of life you live in the present, but the sort of future you are creating for yourself. At one extreme you can live for the moment, gaining maximum pleasure and avoiding pain, regardless of what your behaviour might be storing up for you. At the other extreme you can spend your life preparing for a better future that never happens because you never stop 'saving up' to make it even more pleasurable when it eventually arrives.

Enjoying or enduring?

The first, 'pleasure now and never mind tomorrow' extreme, typically results eventually in circumstances inflicting heavy pain. Thus, if you always do what you enjoy doing, the chances are your boss's objectives, or your spouse's, or even your own longer term interests, may not be met. The resulting 'pain' might be in the form of getting fired, poor health through over-eating, or bankruptcy because you don't like answering official letters. This can easily be averted by using your time more wisely, perhaps accepting a measure of 'pain' for a limited period as an investment in a more predictable and pleasurable future. The other extreme is to endure pain today and every day, which seems to defeat the whole object.

Consumable or investment?

We tend to aim for clearly identified goals or outcomes, and to move towards pleasure and away from pain. This can be converted into a very positive compromise. We can think of time as both a day-to-day consumable (we *spend* it, like buying stationery or food) and also as an investment (like installing double-glazing or building a room in the loft). Viewing time as a consumable, we are likely to try to maximise the pleasure we get in whatever we are doing. Viewing time as an investment,

on the other hand, we also take account of the payback –
outcomes we might enjoy in the future – thus storing up
additional pleasure. The secret is to make your input both –
like eating healthy food (consumable) that you enjoy, and
which also offers long-term health (investment) benefits. The
long-term benefit comes as a free bonus.

In any company or family budget, one kind of expenditure
competes with another. But it's all money – and in the same
way time is time. Each minute we spend can be self-contained,
both an input (to achieve some future outcome) and an output
(the pleasure of doing what you are doing). Or it can have a
meaning outside itself, with a view to higher-level outputs or
outcomes that are likely to be realised in the future. The next
hour, or minute, can have significance – perhaps life-changing
significance – well into the future.

Investing in planning

We also need to invest time planning how we will spend our
time on the tasks or projects themselves. A formal work project
is likely to build in the necessary time for planning, gathering
data and other activities. The temptation with day-to-day
activities, however, is to skip the planning or thinking stage, as
time is so tight. Failure to think ahead is a prime cause of
missed targets – outcomes you fail to achieve – which are
literally a waste of time.

Planning usually forms a big part of time management
books, and I do not intend to repeat the received wisdom. But
with a goal-oriented approach to behaviour there is less risk of
falling into the no-planning trap. Planning, however, can
become an input that is too divorced from its output – a sterile
paper exercise, devoid of imagination and right-brain skills.

Thinking or doing?

A preoccupation with planning reflects a thinking bias. Some
people have an obsession for making lists, resolutions, weekly
or monthly plans, and life blueprints. There is no doubt at all
about the effectiveness of plans, or the benefits of writing them
down, but there is evidence that some people spend time on

planning that could be spent on doing. They are reluctant to move from thinking to acting. Conversely, there are others who jump into action without a thought, only to pay the price for poor preparation. In this case, a small investment in thinking and a simple written plan would bring disproportionate benefits.

Balance, of course is the answer. Peter Drucker, a top management writer, describes the common denominator for all consistently successful people as their perfect balance between thought and action. Planning has to be seen holistically, along with the activity and its outcome, rather than as a watertight part of the process – or worse still, as an end in itself.

Maximising your investment

How do you maximise the planning investment? Just thinking in terms of your goal will go a long way to making clear both the value and also the degree of planning you need. An important letter might justify three or four one-line bullet points of planning – not many seconds of thought – on the purpose of the letter. In the same moments you might also decide whether a letter is the right medium, or whether any communication is needed at all. A couple of minutes on how you are going to express what you want to communicate, to have the best chance of bringing about your desired outcome, will repay itself well. If you don't have an outcome, go back a stage.

Without a purpose, or outcome, you should not have even entered planning mode – you have nothing to plan for. The time investment of planning is an investment in an outcome (output) rather than just a plan for an activity (input). Thankfully, the thought that needs to go into planning will also help to clarify the purpose or outcome, and will involve the goal criteria we met in Chapter 3.

Is planning worth the time spent? An investment of maybe ten per cent of the time that it will take you to carry out a certain activity might mean the difference between achieving your outcome (the purpose of the letter, say) or not. In those terms you cannot afford not to plan. Having said this, if the letter came into your mind when driving to the office and you more or less wrote it 'in your head', your brain has already done some of the planning for you, drawing on the many factors and data that were lying below your conscious mind.

Freewheeling periods

Cultivate these 'downtime', low-focus, 'freewheeling' periods – such as when driving to work, getting dressed and showering, or walking in the park at lunchtime. They are ideal for planning, as well as being enjoyable and sometimes therapeutic. You will find that some of the important thinking processes are optimised, and you save time on the planning process itself.

Planning mode

Just as you can learn the skill of sensory awareness, so you can learn to switch frequently into planning mode. Even a major project might become a workable mental plan while having a long, hot bath. A creative time manager does not stick to rigid 'ten per cent' rules for planning, or any rigid rules. Planning just means thinking ahead, but thinking with your whole brain. It can become a habit, and a way of life, but one we can all develop with practice. It then becomes a blue chip, high-payback investment in sound time management and achievement.

Starters and finishers

You may know already what your bias is when it comes to thinking and doing. Planners spend hours in detailed data gathering and analysis, considering all possible outcomes from different angles. But they leave too little time in which to actually achieve the task, or may procrastinate. The other-type jumps into a task feet first, spending sometimes days without let-up, only to discover they have achieved little. Both have problems managing their time, but for different reasons. One type tends not to start things; the other tends not to finish them.

Tips for 'thinkers' and 'doers'

Having determined your natural style, you can go a long way towards moving it in the direction you choose. If you spend too much time thinking and planning, keep adding 'therefore' to your thoughts.

◆ John is away from the office – therefore I will send a fax now.

◆ The price is too high – therefore I will negotiate now.

◆ The terms of the lease are unclear – therefore I will telephone the lawyer, see Bill about it and fax my queries.

You may feel that you are acting impetuously, but the chances are you will still instinctively plan more than your activist colleagues. Thinking and planning are often convenient cerebral excuses for procrastination. Ask yourself 'What am I going to do – now?'

Alternatively, if you spend too little time thinking and planning ahead, keep asking yourself: Why?

◆ You are about to do a blitz on the filing system after an annoying error you find – why? A wise use of your time, or just getting the frustration out of your system?

◆ Spending hours making telephone calls – why? To achieve sales, maintain important relations, or a poor use of your time?

◆ Speeding down the motorway to keep three appointments – why? Could your outcomes have been achieved in any other way involving less time, effort and money? Or have you always done it that way? If so, why?

In each case ask yourself what the benefits are of doing whatever you are doing. In other words, *stop and think*. It is a useful exercise to write down some of your regular tasks and list the benefits they will bring you. Having done this as a special exercise, the trick then is to develop the Why? technique as a habitual way of thinking. Thinking in any way is just a habit, and it can be changed to serve you better. But it is a wise investment of your time, with a big payback. Done well, it provides jam today and jam tomorrow.

The value you put on your time affects what you do with it and what you ultimately get out of it.

Valuing How You Spend Time

If you want something badly enough, nothing seems to stop you from getting it, and somehow you make time. This simple fact supports the importance of clearly fixing your *outcomes*. Concentrating on outcomes rather than exactly how you will achieve them (the destination rather than the journey) produces results and makes the best use of time. But because we need time to achieve anything worthwhile, it takes on its special value. Time has a value that relates to the value we place on the outcome we want to achieve. This chapter shows how this simple concept of the value of time can be used to increase your productivity.

The opportunity cost of time

The term *opportunity cost* is a useful one. It is the benefit we forgo by taking one course rather than another. If resources, such as money, are scarce, we cannot do everything we would like to. By doing one thing, like going on holiday, we forgo something else, like decorating the bedroom. The opportunity cost of going on holiday is thus decorating the house. Maybe we can afford to do both. Then the opportunity cost of decorating the house might, in turn, be changing the car, buying more presents for the children at Christmas and so on. Our value list would carry on down to cover all the things we might spend our money on, in the order in which we value the benefit we receive.

Time also has a value. Its opportunity cost is:

◆ the value we place on what we might have been doing with it if we were doing something else

◆ and all the benefits that alternative use of time might bring.

Opportunity cost assumes that we do not have infinite resources, and cannot have everything we want, which is a fair assumption for most people. It is particularly relevant when we start to value time, because the supply of time is fixed, and so even scarcer than money and other resources. Like money, time is not much use until you turn it into something else. So its value will relate to the outcomes you can achieve by using it.

A person with no goals is likely to put a low value on their time. A person with big goals will value their time highly, because they can convert it into the pleasure of achievement and fulfilment. So whilst time is in scarce supply, in that it is fixed, its *perceived* value differs dramatically from person to person. And the way you value your time will be a good indication of what you do with it – and what you achieve.

Measuring time

Einstein suggested that time flies when you are enjoying yourself: so the brain must judge the speed of time passing by measuring gaps between moments of enjoyment. For instance, let's say you hate writing reports, but today you must spend all your time writing a monthly report. If your last moment of pleasure was having breakfast or a brief chat when you first came into the office, and your next will be the evening meal or a favourite television programme, the whole day is likely to drag. That is, there is a long time between pleasurable spots in the day. On another day, filled with enjoyable tasks, you can hardly believe your watch when it's time to go home.

All of this makes our preoccupation with time pointless. What we are surely after is to:

◆ achieve more
◆ accomplish more
◆ get pleasure
◆ and avoid pain.

Even if one of your outcomes is 'to have more time for myself', you will have something in mind to do with your time – such as reading, lounging, or going for a walk. That is, you will have a desire or purpose. Time is simply the resource that you need to release it. So we are back to outcomes: identifying them; clarifying them (using the tests of a good outcome); and concentrating on them rather than on filling our time with inputs that will not affect them. In particular, that means knowing the difference between inputs and outputs.

Personal time worth

What does orthodox time management wisdom have to offer? The idea of valuing time is a popular one. Professional people like solicitors and accountants operate on the basis of a rate per hour, which is in effect their value of time. Any of us can do the same thing, as we will all have some value, even if we just think about it when deciding whether it is worth hiring a tradesman, cleaner, decorator, gardener or whoever to do a job we could do ourselves. If we value ourselves more than what it would cost, the chances are we would pay an outsider and use our own time for other things.

There must be more to it. As we have seen, time does not only change its value from person to person, but it changes for the same person in different situations, moods, or even times of the day. You might, for a start, value your time more highly at the weekend than during the week because it is 'yours', while work time belongs to the company, and – just like company cars or pens – it is valued lower. Alternatively, you might value time with your family more highly than time spent socially. Or you might value time spent alone higher than time spent with others – or the other way round.

Quality time

We hear a lot about 'quality time'. But time is time and the distinction, of course, is in what we do with our time, or what we achieve by using it. Quality time with the children probably means doing what is mutually beneficial and pleasurable, rather than just being physically with them. Quality time to yourself probably means not being interrupted, perhaps getting away from familiar surroundings, but most of all doing what to you means quality. So we are back to outcomes, and *what you want*. The value you attach to time will thus relate to how you value the outcome the time enables you to achieve. Get your outcomes right, and in the right order, and time takes care of itself.

The time value flaw

There is a flaw in the 'valuing every hour' technique. If you are a solicitor, the idea is to fill up your diary as much as possible, so that every hour is productive and gives a return at your maximum worth. Perfectly logical. On this basis, given the choice of doing paid overtime or landscaping the garden, if you earn more per hour than it costs to hire a landscape gardener you would probably work the overtime, hire the gardener, and be left with money to go towards a holiday or new clothes, or to save (for future such benefits). Similarly, if you had to choose between decorating the lounge and reading a novel, you would probably choose the decorating, because you would be valuing your time at least at the level it would cost to hire a decorator, and the pleasure of the finished result greater than the pleasure of the finished novel.

On this economic sort of logic certain outcomes will, of course, always justify themselves in our priority ranking. Other activities, like reading, going for a walk, or doing nothing, which are hard to value in monetary terms, are likely to be squeezed right out of our lives. This is in fact what can happen with task-oriented or workaholic people who measure their time in economic terms. They think in quantity rather than quality terms, accepting continuous short-term 'pain' for hoped-for long-term pleasure that never seems to come. Seen holistically, the rationale of squeezing value out of every minute breaks down. On reflection, life is too short and unpredictable for that.

Time spent doing nothing

Let's take another example. How do you value time spent doing nothing? If you don't put a value on it, you will always be doing something, according to the 'valuing time' law. And you might well become a miserable, discontented person in the process. Viewed in outcome terms, however, doing nothing can make more sense. 'Doing nothing' is a figure of speech and we probably mean:

◆ I want to relax and wind down.
◆ I want a completely free weekend.
◆ I want to forget my work for a while.
◆ I want to be free to do anything – read a book, browse through magazines, go for a long walk, have a nap, potter in the garden.

♦ I don't want to *have* to do anything.
♦ I want to catch up on some sleep.
♦ I want to have an evening at home.

That's 'doing nothing' for most people – although we all 'do nothing' differently. The common factor is the perception – in the above cases, probably, of pleasure, or of moving away from pain (facing problems at work, for instance). If doing nothing is perceived as pain ('I'm bored, there's nothing to do'), then it takes on a negative value.

All the above 'outcomes' are valid – your goals don't have to be tangible, material or valuable in money terms. More than that, if you value them higher than other outcomes, like completing a work task, clearing out the garage, or visiting your in-laws, you are *putting a value on time spent doing 'nothing'*.

This is anathema to the time management consultants, because it doesn't make economic sense. However, when we view a person holistically, with feelings and unique perceptions of pleasure, pain and time, rather than as an economic resource, it soon has the ring of common sense.

> The trick is to fulfil more outcomes – to get, do and be what you want – however they stack up economically.

At the same time, decide to get the maximum pleasure out of whatever you are doing moment by moment. Notice that the above examples of doing nothing are typically enjoyable as a process ('being free', 'relaxing', 'doing my thing'), rather than just as an end result ('had a free weekend'). So the rule? Keep your valuing to your outcomes (what you decide you want), and enjoyment of what you do (or don't do), rather than the minutes that will tick away regardless. Try to be content with the standard 24-hours a day you have at your disposal.

Giving time away

A legitimate outcome might be to spend more time with your family, or on a hobby or personal interest. This is likely to pass the outcome tests better than a less specific outcome 'to make my family happy', which is less in your direct control. But do

we value time we 'give away' (such as to people, an
organisation, or a cause)?

Sometimes we are happy to give our time to others for the
pleasure it gives, a sense of duty or loyalty, or whatever. We
have no thought of putting a value on it. In some
circumstances everything becomes secondary to our main
purpose (outcome) and time just has to take care of itself ('I
don't care how long this takes me . . .'). We are free, of course,
to do just what we want with our time – at least with non-
work time. But none of the time management systems I have
come across make room for these 'sovereign' decisions we
make, as human beings, whether rational or irrational.

> Economic-value-driven time management doesn't distin-
> guish between an unwanted incursion into our time and a
> willing offering of our time as part of a loftier personal
> outcome.

Ask yourself: 'What outcomes might suffer if my spouse,
children and close friends had to justify an hourly rate when
calling upon my time?' Time can easily become our master,
rather than the priceless resource and ally that it is.

Another aspect of time management, therefore, is
reconciling your own free choice and pleasure with the many
demands that come from outside. Otherwise work and modern
life will become a treadmill. As we have seen, by thinking in
outcome terms – whether those outcomes are quantifiable or
just qualitative – time takes care of itself. The very busiest
people seem to be able to find time for things they consider
important, whether or not they have been neatly scheduled into
their lives. They seem more ready than others to give of their
time freely and, amazingly, never seem the worse off.

Standard ration

The fixed nature of time does make it a special resource, even
more universally valued than money. Other than the couple of
hours' difference either way that each of us spend in sleep, we
all have a standard ration. Whilst some people can have an
unfair advantage in life by choosing the right parents or being

specially gifted in some way, time is an egalitarian resource. It is also the most convertible. The solicitor or consultant can convert it into money, or any of us can convert it into a neat lawn, a tidy desk, an academic degree, a better figure and countless other pleasurable outcomes. But the monetary analogy soon breaks down. Time can heal wounds that no amount of money can. And time has a unique value for another reason. You can't save it up for a rainy day. When it's spent, it's gone forever. Recognise time as your scarcest, most convertible asset, and you will begin to value it as it deserves to be valued.

CHAPTER 9

Priorities, Outcomes and Motivation

A t the level of daily and weekly jobs it is important to give further thought to priorities. These tasks might be routine and menial, and tend to be quite specific, but without them we are unlikely to produce anything worthwhile. Several such tasks might be required to support a very worthy longer-term outcome. So which do you do first? Equally important, which is sacrificed altogether if time runs out? This chapter applies some 'right-brain thinking' to priority setting and suggests changes that take account of you as a total person, how you feel and what motivates you.

Testing outcomes

We have already seen the importance of setting priority ranking to tasks. The main test is whether our task, or whatever we are going to spend our time on, will bring about some outcome. It is as well to list our goals first, as we saw in Chapter 3, as otherwise we tend to invent goals afterwards to justify how we have already spent our time. This is a fact of human nature. We do some things because we enjoy doing them and the only outcome they produce is the pleasure of doing them – the input. That's fine if you are not concerned about achieving anything, or investing for bigger benefits in the future. You will never achieve anything if you spend your time on inputs not directed towards outputs. But the idea of goal orientation is simple, and is a natural process you can bring under your control. Just thinking about outcomes usually throws up priorities. We naturally spend our time according to how we rate the outcomes we are working towards.

Another rule is to make sure your goals are clear, specific and 'real' by applying the various simple tests in Chapter 3.

This usually results in changes that increase the chances of success. Some jobs have to be made (to seem) bigger, others smaller. Deadlines may need to be changed. You may have to sort out competing objectives.

> Some unrealistic or unmotivating goals may disappear altogether, but it is unlikely you would have achieved them anyway and you can spend your time on more realistic, robust outcomes.

The goal-testing process usually results in a natural ranking of your goals, as you visualise the evidence of success and are motivated to achieve. Priorities emerge as you plan and think about what you want to achieve. It is not just a cold, logical exercise. Even at the planning stage it involves how you feel and the extent to which you are motivated to see the job through to completion.

Rationing outcomes

We usually have a lot more things we want to do than we can ever hope to achieve. So while setting priorities you will need to do some *goal rationing* – just as when you have to reconcile your monthly income with what you want to spend. This need not be a negative exercise. You will be left with the goals that you value the highest, give you the most pleasure, and (having applied the 'tests') have the best chance of realisation.

Realistic rationing is a form of investment. Managing your time better will mean that you will be looking to achieve more and bigger goals next year and further into the future. You learn to succeed rather than fail – and succeeding is a better way to use your time. As well as having a better chance of success, by rationing your goals you will focus on what is most important, and not spread your motivation too thinly. In fact, the exercise is not to ration time but *outcomes*. Time takes care of itself. Maximum motivation occurs when you direct all your effort into outputs you have specifically chosen and value highly.

What if? questions

You can focus on the important jobs by posing 'what if?' and other questions to yourself:

- What if I could only do three tasks this week? What would they be?
- What if I had only an hour to spend, what would I spend it on?
- If I had to spend time in hospital from next week, what would I have to clear up before then? And how would I best achieve that?
- If I had access to the best scientists and thinkers in the world, what sort of questions would I put to them regarding this task?
- What sort of answers might they give?
- If I was certain I could not fail in this job, how might I act differently?

In this way your imaginative right brain produces scenarios, mind pictures, seeds of thought or half-ideas. In the process priorities fall into place and motivation is born.

One of the outcome tests we applied in Chapter 3 concerned the scale of the goals or tasks. Besides ensuring that you are properly motivated with the right level of challenge, you have to get your jobs into a format that is amenable for weekly and daily tasks. Big time chunks – even if you are confident you can cope with the job personally – will have less chance of success in the face of the distraction and outside factors most of us face.

Important or urgent

Let's see what can be done further about ranking jobs you would typically schedule daily and weekly. The ranking distinction is identified in every time management textbook, and relates to what is urgent and what is important. When planning your time, the chances are that although each goal has some importance, few issues will be really urgent. Most of our use of time tends to be in reaction to outside pressures, demands and requests, and we often accept that something is urgent at face value. A colleague who is assertive will soon make you feel his request is urgent. The skill in discriminating between what is urgent and what is important is one that comes into its own in the heat of life and dealings with other people, rather than when reflectively setting your periodic goals. Behavioural skills rather than logical systems are needed to get control of your life and time, and you often need intuition and a sixth sense.

Self-generated urgency

There are exceptions. You may have been procrastinating about one of your main outcomes for a while, and a time fuse is ticking. Soon it becomes urgent, it ranks high on your list. Another justification of the urgent label is when there is plenty of time to go on a bigger, important job, and you are reluctant to make a start for whatever reason. To overcome the inertia of making a start you may have to treat the getting-off-the-ground stage as urgent. Otherwise, that is what it will become soon and you may then have less control than now. Doing such a task need not interfere with 'real' urgent jobs, as making a start often takes up very little time. For example, a single telephone call or fax might start a process which you will then be more likely to continue, especially if other people become involved and further procrastination would mean a loss of face.

Who says it is urgent?

What about tasks that are classified as urgent by others? The first rule is that urgency is in the eye of the beholder. It is a highly subjective and often irrational concept. Secondly, urgency is ephemeral. Often you (or your boss) can't even remember a task, let alone why you thought it was urgent. Statistically most 'urgent' communications, if not responded to for example, will result in no further communication or no outcome at all. Really urgent matters are usually followed up by a telephone call or some other intervention anyway. So it works out that, on average, you will not die or even be fired for not treating every everything described as urgent with urgency.

The urgent label does not mean the task is exempt from the outcome test – 'What is being achieved, what is the output?' Typically, in the heat of the moment, an urgent job takes on a life of its own, and its achievement becomes an end in itself. On reflection it may have nothing to do with your main objectives. If it does contribute it may be the wrong (inefficient, slow, expensive) way to achieve those objectives. Or it might be in the nature of an input task that is not producing outputs for anyone – and certainly not contributing to the higher-level objectives of you or your organisation.

Diminishing returns

Another universal rule that applies to managing time is the law of diminishing returns. A single underlining graduates to a three-line-whip, then a coloured 'urgent' label, then all sorts of tricks are used to grab attention, as professional debt collectors know well. In the end just about everything has to be called 'urgent' or it will not get any attention at all. A true time manager sees through this tendency and stays in control. Whilst recognising role, power and politics, particularly in an employment context, the urgent/important distinction is one you have to make for yourself. It is the basis of personal time management.

You decide

Whenever possible, you should decide on what is urgent. You are free to accept your boss's classification, of course, and to unilaterally change or disregard it might be career limiting. But at least be aware of your choice and the effect of any decision on your time. The rhetoric of an 'urgent' memo rarely reflects the true urgency of a situation, at least in terms of you and your outcomes. Start to take responsibility for what is urgent and how you spend your time. In the longer term a manager, for instance, who takes this line is more likely to gain respect and promotion. Dire consequences can result from trying to respond to every call on your time.

You are still left with the job of fixing your own priorities, whether in reacting to claims of urgency and importance, or in setting your own goals and allocating time to them. Judgement as well as behavioural skills, such as assertiveness, is called upon. Recognising what is likely to *become* urgent, in particular, is a skill that requires a whole brain perspective. That's not easily trainable in a conventional sense. It involves intuition, rather than a narrow, logical focus, to appreciate the subtle and probably diverse possibilities. Successful time managers describe this as a sort of sixth sense. Whatever it is, it is a holistic way of thinking of which we are all capable.

Urgency and the meta model

The so-called Meta Model in neuro-linguistic programming is a useful language pattern to improve information, and clarify otherwise general or distorted communications. It identifies common patterns of language (about a dozen) such as 'universal quantifiers' that comprise absolute terms like 'always' and 'never', spurious 'cause and effect' statements, and other generalisations and distortions of meaning. The idea of questioning loosely-framed 'surface level' language can be applied in many ways, and might help in better thinking about urgent tasks that invade our time.

Urgent responses

Lumbered with an 'urgent' task, simple responses will usually expose an ill-thought-out or selfish 'urgent' label:

◆ What exactly is the purpose of this?
◆ What if it was done next month?
◆ What would happen if . . .?
◆ Why?
◆ Who says so?
◆ How does this relate to the divisional results (further up a hierarchy of goals that we met in Chapter 3)?
◆ Need it be urgent every month?
◆ How can we all avoid urgency in the future?
◆ How does it rank in urgency against so-and-so?

The language of a response to an 'urgent' demand will differ, of course, as between a subordinate, close relative and the company chairman. But the principle of 'insightful' responses remains, if you are to have any control over your own time. Shallow or fuzzy language usually signals sloppy thinking, and poorly thought out goals – as well as poor use of time on the part of somebody. Legitimate functional and company objectives, of course, *become* your own (because that's your job), and may be incorporated into a job description (usually open, however, to some negotiation). So you will have a sound 'outcome basis' against which to test tasks as they come along. If not, it might be a wise investment of your time to get agreement about what job, departmental or company goals you are responsible for.

The whole range of Meta Model patterns can elicit scores of new perspectives to help understanding and communication (see Further Reading). For the moment get into the habit of questioning any call upon your time – asking the sort of questions above – in relation to your own goals and values. If you decide to take a goal on board, subject it to the goal tests in Chapter 3.

Stick to your outcome guns

From time to time you may have to amend your outcomes temporarily: 'Keep managing director happy at all costs', for example, or 'Keep in John's good books at least until after the appraisal.' Or you may have to engineer a change in your own job description, and job targets. That is your choice, whatever the implicit risks. But usually an unreasonable request for urgency has no basis other than the assertiveness of the communicator, misuse of rank, or at best somebody's *perception* of urgency. It will rarely fit the key criteria against which you are measured as an employee or manager, let alone the outcomes you set for yourself.

So stick to your outcome guns. Every battle won or lost makes the outcome of the time management war – one way or the other – more certain. Today's business leaders learnt to manage their time long before they reached the pinnacle of their organisation and had no more bosses to contend with.

Whose goal, anyway?

The question of 'whose goals am I fulfilling, anyway?' keeps cropping up in time management, especially in employer/ employee relationships. It also appears in non-work situations, although it is usually less obvious. Your goal, for example, might be what your daughter or grandchild wants. That is, you are happy to subsume your desires to theirs. But however worthy our intentions, and whilst parents want the best for their child academically or professionally, most such outcomes are more in the child's control than the parent's.

As 'well-formed outcomes', subsumed goals don't score well. This doesn't mean that goals on behalf of others have to be abandoned. All sorts of goals within your control might *help towards* the outcomes of other people for whom you are concerned. You can only do what *you* can do. Provided they meet the other criteria about being specific and amenable to evidence, these personal goals can be set with confidence.

Work goals

In some senses work goals are easier to get right, as they are often formalised into your job description. Certain tasks and responsibilities are legitimately delegated to you, and should contribute to higher-level departmental or company objectives. Outcomes are less clear domestically and socially, and often you are lumbered with all sorts of responsibilities by default. The main dilemma in a work situation is when the goals in question do not bring you the pleasure required of a motivating goal – as would automatically be the case for a personal goal concerning your family, or a work goal that you have set yourself.

In many cases, fortunately, there is inherent pleasure in *just doing a good job*, whatever it might be, and especially if it requires a degree of professionalism. In extreme cases, however, you might have to think about whether you are right to stick with the job. Work can be a treadmill of perceived pain. Even when you manage your time well and achieve your goals, you get no real sense of fulfilment. In the present climate of almost universal job insecurity, the 'final' option is not as far-fetched as it once was. More practically, aspects of your work can usually be renegotiated.

Try it now   There is also the option of changing how you think about your job. Think of the job you dislike most. Then, in a relaxed, brainstorming mood:

- Think of three ways to do the job in less time.
- Think of three ways to do it in the same time, but in a different way.
- Decide on three rewards that might make you think differently about doing the job.
- Think of three things about the job that are not too bad.
- Think of something about it that is pleasant or acceptable.
- Imagine what it would be like doing the job if you enjoyed doing it (if you think that's stupid, imagine it isn't).
- Imagine how you would feel if you could do the job in half the time.
- Think of three ways you could get someone else to do the job.
- Think of what would happen if you did not do the job.
- Visualise yourself doing the job, but change some visual submodalities (see Chapter 6).
- Imagine doing the job but change some of the voices or other sounds.
- Run through the job in your mind but add some funny or bizarre changes.
- Check back to your hierarchy of goals and identify which of them will be helped by the successful completion of this job.

Using your sixth sense

Many decisions about what is important and what is urgent are far from simple, and may not fit logical decision-making processes. Judgement rather than logic may be needed to spot the fake urgent jobs, as we saw earlier, and the really important ones. This is where the unconscious right-brain comes in. How we spend our time might reveal some unconscious intention – say, to be liked. Although not listed as a goal, this 'intention' is nonetheless as real as any conscious one, and just as powerful in motivating our behaviour. It can affect our response to requests, our relationship with bosses and subordinates, our use of time and money, and indeed all our interpersonal dealings.

We therefore need to be more aware of these unconscious intentions. If we agree they are valid and consistent with our other goals, we can build them into our use of time. We also need to start using some intuition (or manifestation of our unconscious mind) in decisions about how we use our time, and particularly in identifying and ranking 'important' and 'urgent' tasks. Many such decisions are far from black and white, and we need to call on a sort of sixth sense to decide wisely, especially if we need to make a fast decision.

Having a feel for the situation

Successful people seem to have the ability to judge in these situations. In most cases they describe the process as intuitive rather than logical. For example, they might describe 'having a feel' for a situation, or they just *know* that something is liable to blow up before long, if not handled promptly. No spreadsheet or computer system can replace common sense and judgement in these everyday decisions. Nor is anyone incapable of the mental skills of intuition – it is as universal a human resource as is imagination. And it can be improved with use. That means:

◆ Taking risks from time to time in the absence of all the information you would ideally want.
◆ Getting to know your unconscious mind.
◆ Improving the quality of insights.
◆ Being as decisive about how you use your time as about anything else.
◆ Using all the intuitive brain support you can command.

Intuition is a key factor in the success of business leaders. They have managed to solve the number one management issue: managing their time; managing themselves. That's why they are able to occupy present leadership positions. Lack of intuitive mental skills is a feature of mediocrity in all spheres of life. In organisations it is a conspicuous factor lower down the management hierarchy. It is not surprising that organisations continue to function after whole layers of middle management are culled. However – and this is the good news – this and other right-brain skills can be learnt and developed. It is largely a process of *self*-development. Trust your unlimited mental powers in more and more situations. Start, if you wish, with decisions that will not have life and death consequences, and build up your self-trust as you gain a track record of successful, sound judgement. Hours – even minutes – will have a new significance as you learn to operate at your best.

Questioning insight

The importance of this sixth sense cannot be overemphasised. This is the skill that spots, sometimes in an instant, a crucial factor that might not have got any attention at all. Right-brain thinking recognises 'burning fuses' – telltale signs about issues that will become urgent all too soon. It is the holistic part of our thinking that sees different perspectives in a situation, and it is these perspectives that form the truths or insights upon which many quality decisions are based. If you have the time and resources to retrospectively check out your intuition, fine; but that is a luxury. It is a wiser investment to hone up your intuitive skills. If simple logic or a computer program can produce the answer, you don't need your sixth sense.

Beware, though, as 'questioning insight' must stand alongside the rationale of any decision about how you use your time. Your personal ranking of outcomes is too important to hand over to a system – even if one could be found. But you have a remarkable *internal* ranking system – intuition, judgement, common sense, or however it is termed. That's the basis of super productivity – of doing twice as much in half the time – and a sense of personal fulfilment into the bargain.

Mental freewheeling

In my discussions with top leaders, many described how ideas would come to them when driving the car, mowing the lawn, or perhaps when jogging. With no planned agenda, apparently random thoughts transform into eureka-type solutions and at other times with better questions or a better sense of perspective. One of the most remarkable aspects of this freewheeling type of thinking is the way the subconscious seems to present to the surface issues that are truly important to a person, but which might be missed – forever – at a conscious level. Such thoughts, desires and ideas might not rank high, nor even appear, on a to-do list. Yet they emerge, as if on cue and in accordance with a master purpose, in the freewheeling mental journey when we are in a relaxed state.

> Getting your priorities right, whether in top leadership, in the family, or in personal self-fulfilment, is central to success, and certainly to making the best use of your time.

And priorities are not subject to any known logic or management system. Who has not woken during the night, captivated by an idea to which they would never have given attention on any rational basis? Who has not received a solution from nowhere, even when their back was to the wall and there seemed to be no way out? Anecdotally, at least, the impact of these 'thinking times' is dramatic. It affects how we use our time and whether we succeed or fail. If we were not so conditioned to left-brain thinking, and outdated, mediocre self-beliefs, this would not come as any surprise.

The Pareto trap

The Pareto 80/20 rule, when applied to inputs and outputs that we have already discussed, typically means that 80 per cent of our effort or input produces just 20 per cent of our output. This is often shown as an effort/results curve. The same curve (see Figure 12) illustrates the equally universal law of diminishing returns: each extra increment of effort (input) produces less and less output. In terms of priority ranking, the 'rule' illustrates how badly we get it wrong, minutiae taking the place of important outcomes.

The idea of right-brain creativity is to reverse this incremental struggle for output. The intuition, eurekas, and 'not trying too hard' of creative thinking produce maximum output with minimum input. So the curve is reversed (see Figure 13).

Pareto's law is hard to avoid even with the most meticulous time planning. But we have already gone a long way to correcting this imbalance, by stressing the importance of outputs. It is simply because we do not take account of our objectives, but think instead about how we are filling our time – inputs – that we succumb to the Pareto trap.

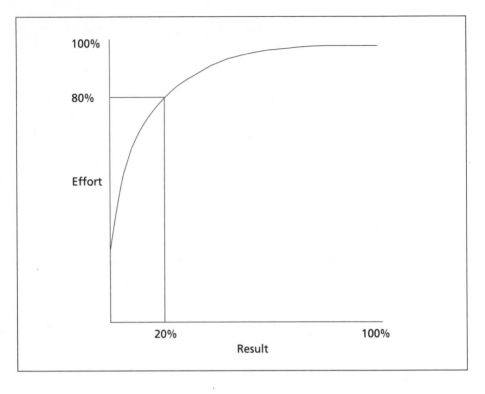

Fig. 12. Effort/result curve.

How to avoid the Pareto trap

Here's how to avoid that trap and reverse the effort/results curve in your own life:

- ◆ Agree your goals and apply the tests in Chapter 3.
- ◆ Identify inputs and outputs.
- ◆ Eliminate activities that are not contributing to chosen outputs.
- ◆ Look at things from new angles; turn things on their head (see also Chapter 13).
- ◆ Think first in terms of radical changes to what you do rather than tinkering at the edges (for instance halving the time it takes, eliminating an activity altogether, or taking an entirely different approach to the problem).
- ◆ Identify your top few important goals and give these your thinking time, including time for incubation.
- ◆ Operate in your mastery and challenge zones for optimum performance.

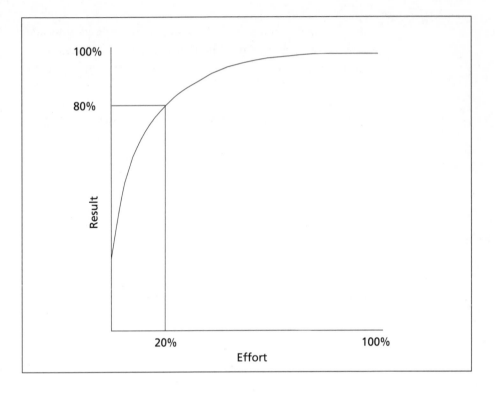

Fig. 13. Effort/result curve, reversed.

Falling off the bottom of the list

We perpetually push important output tasks off the bottom of our priority list. This is what the 'easy first' school of thought promotes (get rid of the easy things first). It is a recipe not just for bad time management, but also for sheer incompetence. Work that is central to our outcomes is replaced by enjoyable but ineffectual inputs. Put bluntly, the two out of ten (20 per cent) outputs that we spend most of our time (80 per cent) achieving, remain at the bottom of the list and never get done. So these natural 'rules' combine to spell non-performance. Even with the best will in the world (and we have seen how little left-brain 'will' has to do with it) important outcomes can be despatched to oblivion.

In some cases the situation is even worse, in that some effort is put into a task, but it is never completed. The inputs might be high, but the real outputs remain zero. In time management terms this is worse than not attempting to do anything in the first place, as scarce time has been used to no avail. So our outcome must become a fixation. We cannot rely on the crutches of techniques and systems: our thinking has to change.

> Once you take control and start to choose what outcomes you will pursue, and what you will do with your time to achieve them, you start using the 80/20 rule to your benefit.

You consciously opt for minimum effort (input) and maximum result (output), as Figure 13 illustrates.

Improving your 'to-do' list

The principles and laws about setting priorities can be used to improve the effectiveness of any to-do list – whatever 'system' you use. It usually comes back to motivation.

There are different schools of thought as to whether we should tackle the easy jobs first, or start with the hard ones. We have already discussed the distinction between urgent and important. If you start with hard ones the danger is that you will get bogged down and never reach those at the bottom of your list. But if you do the easy ones first, the chances are that the hard ones will never get done, as we tend to be over-optimistic in listing too many jobs anyway, as well as underestimating how long tasks will take.

◆ By doing the hard tasks first we have an inbuilt incentive in that we will get to do the easy ones when those are complete, and they act as 'reward' (like leaving your favourite food to the end).

◆ By introducing *contrived* rewards – in this case just by changing the order of tasks – you tap into your pleasure-seeking tendency and will use time more wisely.

Hard-to-easy ranking

How do you avoid getting bogged down in an early, difficult task? The answer is to 'chunk' down the tasks into more manageable ones that are well within your ability. Each difficult but manageable task can be followed by a built-in reward, just big enough to motivate you to get on with the difficult task and also to do it quickly – to make better use of your scarce time. Alternatively one of the easier jobs (just one) can be brought forward as a sort of downpayment, before you carry on with the next most difficult task for the day. This token task should be short – maybe just five minutes or so – rather than an extended one. You can reserve bigger but enjoyable tasks as *major rewards* when you have cleared up the distasteful, important ones.

So the general principle is 'hard to easy', but using rewards throughout, and slightly amending the *order* of tasks to ensure maximum motivation. Time management is about doing good deals between:

◆ your logical and intuitive mind
◆ pleasure and pain
◆ the long-term and the short-term.

Pleasure-to-pain ranking

Another way to classify your day's tasks is according to the perceived pleasure and perceived pain involved (in the doing of the job, that is, rather than in the outcome, or benefits you will achieve having completed it). It is possible, of course, that technically the hardest job gives you the most pleasure – maybe because you enjoy working with numbers or have particular experience, or the challenge itself provides pleasure. Maybe you enjoy doing new things. These are useful self-motivators.

Similarly, the easiest of tasks might be boring and distasteful. In these cases the pleasurable jobs – whether 'easy' or 'difficult' – act as their own incentives, so it makes sense to leave them until you have done the others. Even when overloaded with work, we rarely fail to do the jobs we enjoy. In fact we unconsciously gravitate towards them just like going for chocolates when depressed. So there is little danger of them getting shoved into the future indefinitely.

You then have an inbuilt motivator, just by changing the order of tasks you would have to do anyway. So here the principle is 'painful to pleasurable', which may override the 'hard to easy' rule. In both cases you use rewards and minor changes to the ranking to keep you going.

By understanding how our brain works we can rank any tasks according to their pleasure/pain rating, using the pleasurable ones as motivators to complete the others. Tackling the difficult/distasteful ones first then makes sense, as again, we can soon handle a technically easy but distasteful task if called upon to do so (like swallowing a small pill). Or we can resort to a contrived form of reward. We are probably at our most productive during the early part of the day in any event, so it is sound time management wisdom to get the worst out of the way (hard and distasteful) when we are operating at peak physical and mental levels.

The best motivator

The best motivator for how we use our time, however, is the outcome we will achieve. So the best test of any to-do list is the extent to which each task fits into your overall hierarchy of goals. The goal hierarchy exercise will also eliminate tasks that you should not be doing. Linked with your goals and values exercise (Chapter 4) it will also suggest which tasks are most important, and thus their priority ranking.

Simply following the process will, in fact, generate motivation, as you think about the higher outcomes and imagine the extra benefits successful completion of the tasks will lead to. Interim rewards are just 'little outcomes' that help to get us started or keep us going. In the case of long-term goals these mini-outcomes are only necessary because the ultimate outcomes are not real (or sensory) enough in our imagination. Or we perceive them as being too far into the future, and discount their value. By using the visualisation techniques described earlier we can enhance those images, and thus strengthen them as internal goals.

Many of our day-to-day actions are based on the association and choices we make unconsciously that reflect our internally fixed goals – our intentions and purposes. There is a limit to what your conscious, logical mind can do in making better use of time, especially when you have tried several times before. In theory you just need willpower. But in practice you need:

◆ imagination
◆ intuition

◆ ingenuity
◆ and belief in yourself.

The whole mind can do extraordinary feats of creative thinking
and problem-solving, mostly in ways that we have not begun to
understand, but to a large extent can stimulate and harness.
What you do with your time can pay big dividends.

You can gain a lot by utilising unconscious brain processes towards achieving conscious goals.

Uptime, Downtime and Focus

A post-mortem on our use of time would be likely to illustrate enormous gaps between what we intended and what we actually did. We are easily distracted from what we know to be important. In the heat of the moment we just forget. We lose focus, or concentration, on the job in hand. This is more so when we do not have much control over our time and are frequently interrupted by others. But it also applies when we have time to ourselves, yet seem to get sucked into new thoughts and minor diversions.

Whenever we carry out an intensive, demanding activity, such as (for most people) making a short speech, we need to be focused. A special one-minute presentation, for instance, if you are to communicate effectively, will require your mind to be fully on the job in hand. We usually prepare for such special events, get ourselves 'psyched up', and are very conscious of what we are thinking and doing.

Similarly, if you are given a big, challenging task with 15 minutes in which to do it, somehow you manage to focus your thinking and energy on the job in hand. As with the 'going on holiday' miracle, you produce a far greater output than you would normally have achieved in such a short period. When you are mentally absorbed in this way you may even forget major domestic or other outside things that might normally have distracted you. Everything goes into the immediate job in hand.

There are other times when we are preoccupied and our thoughts wander. This chapter explains what is known as the '*thinking spectrum*', and suggests ways in which you can, on the one hand, keep focused, but where necessary engage in low-focus, or lateral thinking to maximise your creativity.

Uptime and downtime

At times of high concentration you are in what is called 'uptime'. Your thoughts are operating at a very focused, conscious level. The opposite state is 'downtime', in which the mind wanders, preoccupied with other things, and loses track of time. At any time we operate at high focus (uptime), low focus (downtime), or somewhere in between. And this has everything to do with how we use our time, and how effective we are.

Conscious uptime is characteristic of left-brain thinking, and what we normally associate with ordinary 'thinking'. But it is only the tip of the iceberg in relation to what the brain does. It is not the only way of thinking, and in many situations, not the most effective. If you are trying to remember the name of a friend from years ago, for example, the chances are that by concentrating hard you will make the task even more difficult. By thinking about something completely different, however, the name is likely to come to you in a flash. Paradoxically, for most people, this right-brain way of thinking, which lets the unconscious brain do the work, is also *quicker* than left-brain trying. Sometimes you struggle with a problem consciously half through the night. So this has obvious time management implications.

> We need to know when and how to focus to get the best out of our time, but also when and how to operate in 'downtime', if that is more appropriate.

The idea of focus, or alertness, is a familiar one. When in a foreign country or at a special concert or sporting event we often want to take in everything about it – to 'savour the moment'. We do this in a heightened state of focus or awareness. Successful time managers, once they have decided on something, concentrate fully on the job in hand, seeming to live fully in the 'now', and making every second count. This is uptime, characterised by mental alertness and a high state of consciousness. Once you have set your outcome and know just what has to be done, you need to allocate prime, uninterrupted time, keep focused and make the most of every moment.

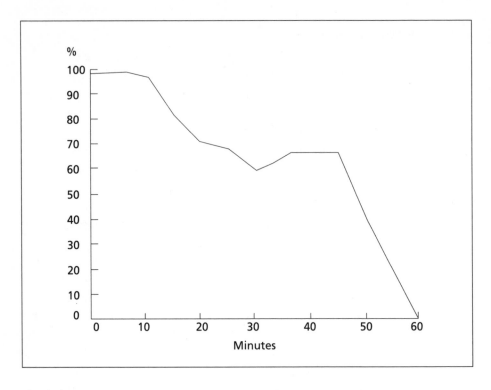

Fig. 14. Concentration span.

Keeping your attention

When thinking in this focused way, you are in full control and are able to manage your time well. It is unusual to be constantly in such a state, however, and high achievers seem to need time to relax and let their hair down. Long periods of high focus are draining. We cannot stay long at peak focus level without reducing our output – not least due to fatigue. Figure 14 shows how quickly our concentration falls off after about three-quarters of an hour.

One time management objective, therefore, is to have plenty of alert *periods*, however short and difficult to arrange, using these to achieve specific, planned outcomes. How do we create such moments?

Planning for high-focus time

It comes down to planning, and in particular, arranging not to be interrupted or distracted. Planning relates not just to the time we need to do a job, and the right environment, but also to setting the outcome, or goal, itself. The goal should be clear and sufficiently motivating to maintain our focus for the necessary period. You can't force yourself to concentrate for long on something that is of no interest. Conversely, you can stay absorbed in a hobby or enjoyable work project for hours, defying all the 'rules' about concentration span and even fatigue. So we are back to motivation, and the importance of prioritising, which we have already discussed.

◆ If you have not sorted out what is urgent and what is important, your mind is likely to wander (to what *is*, to you, important).

◆ Knowing up front the importance and order of tasks means you can give them your full attention and enthusiasm.

So much can be accomplished in this focused state that it should not be necessary to encroach on quality downtime, which is time for relaxing or daydreaming, and building up energy, perhaps keeping fit, creating new outcomes by visualisation, or allowing thoughts to incubate. But it does take some discipline and practice. Although we may intend to stay focused, our mind gets diverted because we are either tackling more than one job at once, are not sufficiently motivated by the task in hand, or our concentration is interrupted.

Tasks competing for your attention

Imagine you have two important tasks, among others, for the day. First you need to draft an important report – call it Job 1. For this you will need to be very alert, to call upon all your professional skills – memory, reasoning powers and language. It may take about an hour. Job 2 will take about ten minutes. It is more urgent than the report, although you can easily rattle it off straight after lunch in good time for the 3 o'clock deadline. This task also needs concentration, albeit for a shorter period. Because of the people it involves, Job 2 is also 'politically charged'. Job 1 is likely to be as enjoyable as it is challenging. Job 2 is a bit distasteful and an unwelcome intrusion into your day. It is also something that you think would have been better handled by your boss.

What happens? While trying to focus on the report your mind, so often a law unto itself, is diverted to the second job. The emotion linked with the afternoon deadline and brief presentation invades your scheduled hour. You can't get your mind round the complex issues in the report, going over the same sentence again and again. In fact you are handling two important jobs at the same time, even though you did not set out to. And neither is done well.

Allocating high-focus time

Understanding the principles of uptime and downtime, how might you have used your time better? You could have focused on Job 2 first, and got rid of it in the ten minutes it would have taken, before getting down to the longer report. But even had you done so you might well have continued to think about it through the morning. In particular, you might have worried about the response when you came to present it, how so-and-so might react, and what the other implications might be. In this case you might realise it was interfering with the job in hand and try to clear your mind. But the harder you try the harder it is to focus on the report. By lunchtime you wonder whether it was even worth starting the thing – you are no clearer in your mind about the main points and conclusion than you had been the night before. And you are not sure at all whether you are ready when 3 o'clock comes round. Each time the issues go through your mind different possibilities are thrown up and different emotions arise.

When allocating high focus time, you need to take account of the nature of the task, not just the technical inputs and the number of minutes it will take. As we saw in the example, a 'ten-minute job' can ruin a morning.

Allowing for emotion

This is where self-awareness comes in. We know ourselves quite well, and will probably know when tasks or issues are likely to vie for our attention.

◆ Can you 'put it to bed', or will it demand further thinking attention?

◆ Will the task be naturally motivating, or do you need to build in a reward or some other driver?
◆ Is it emotionally charged, or can you confine it to neat, left-brain boundaries?

We can usually guess, for instance, those jobs that are emotionality charged. They sometimes involve difficult people, and are likely to demand precedence. Some tasks we tend to worry about, both before and after, whilst others we take in our stride. So a bit of sensible rescheduling is called for. 'Rules' (like easy first or hard first) may have to be aborted (a 'rule' of creative time management). In this case, to settle down to Job 1 after Job 2 might have made more sense. But this could only be after the 3 o'clock presentation when the task, its worries and unknowns, were out of your hair.

Rearranging for mental breaks

Alternatively, it might have been wiser to slot in another short task – maybe one involving a visit to another office or the plant – as a mental break to get into the empowering state needed for the report. Perhaps the timing of Job 2 was negotiable, so the scheduled report-writing hour need not be changed. Perhaps the job itself was negotiable. What was the purpose of the short task? What would happen after your recommendation? Was there another way to have achieved the outcome? Or might the main work on the report have been better done on Sunday morning? Presumably you could choose when to do such a task over a period of days if not weeks, in which case you would surely schedule it either after a Job 2 type task or, better still, on a day when you wouldn't have any special diversions.

There are no rights or wrongs, but knowing the vital need to concentrate on the job in hand, and our vulnerability to all sorts of distractions, a better way is usually there for the taking. A lot of executives, whilst not giving up undue amounts of leisure time, know which jobs are best carried out away from the distractions of the busy work environment.

Outside interruptions

In the cases I have used, the loss of focus could not be blamed on a boss or inconsiderate colleague, or even an uncomfortable chair. It involved a mental distraction. But focus might well have been lost as a result of an interruption from outside – a well-meaning colleague with a matter of his or her own that demanded your brief but undivided attention. Obviously focus can be lost in all sorts of ways, but if you are aware of this you don't need prescriptions to solve your problem. Rather, you need the determination to get it right next time, and a desire to foster better longer-term thinking habits.

We have seen that using time to the best involves a preoccupation with outcomes. Among other things this reduces the chance of doing the wrong thing, but it also involves doing things in the right way in the light of how you think and work best as an individual.

> Just like physical interruptions, mental 'competition' reduces your focus, and you need to remember this when planning your time.

When you lose focus, not only can you not concentrate on the job in hand and thus work efficiently, but you lose track of time anyway.

Activities that produce outputs in a controlled space of time are best carried out in uptime. Once in high focus, you will amaze yourself at what you can achieve. This is an important dimension to your time management skills. Do everything necessary to your environment and schedule to prevent interruptions and get the quality time periods you need.

Try it now

List your jobs for tomorrow, or for the coming week, using the priority principles we looked at in the last chapter. Now apply the focus criterion – decide which jobs, or which part of your tasks, require high-focus uptime. Allocate periods that are short enough to ensure you will be free from interruptions, but long enough to do justice to the phase of the job or specific task. Decide upon a maximum time period for any task or phase of a task. Then rearrange the order of your tasks so that you can imagine yourself giving full attention as you move from one job to another. Make sure there are gaps in between for downtime, when you can relax and let your mind wander, or think about upcoming tasks in a relaxed, freewheeling mode.

Cultivating alertness

Alertness has other more general benefits. 'Sensory acuity' is part of the cycle of goal achievement and success generally that we touched on earlier. It also involves alertness and powers of observation. One way to be more observant, and to stay alert, is to change your routines. Whenever you are on 'autopilot', carrying out activities without thinking, you are prone to let your mind wander, and are less aware of what is going on in the immediate, sensory world.

Try it now

Make a list of ways you can change your routines. Here are some examples, but a little creativity will produce scores of ideas:

◆ Get dressed in a different sequence.
◆ Change your route to work.
◆ Eat at different places for lunch.
◆ Read different books from usual.
◆ When walking through the plant or office, imagine you are someone else – perhaps a customer or supplier – and note how it feels. Notice the sort of things they would notice, and comments they might make.
◆ In a meeting watch people's hands, or eyes, relating what you see to what they are saying. Note who says most, and who stays quiet.
◆ Do something different yourself, like avoiding criticism, or making excuses.

Choose a short-list of items that will produce plenty of change but that are realistic, can be introduced immediately, and that you think you will enjoy. Also choose a mixture on daily, weekly and longer-term routines. Now decide what action is needed (1) in the next hour, (2) tomorrow, (3) next week, (4) next month.

On putting your changes into practice become aware of the

new sights, sounds and feelings you experience. Be open to new ideas and opportunities to help you bring about your outcomes.

The exercise above will help to cultivate alertness, and will help when you need to concentrate for more important reasons – like writing a major report. You will learn to direct your thinking and behaviour in a highly conscious way, concentrating if necessary for long periods. The different perspectives these private 'games' offer might well throw up valuable ideas on any current problems, so your time will be well spent.

The mind is attracted to novelty, and new routines will disrupt mental as well as physical habits. However, this can also involve stress – we don't like change in big measure. So make any changes gradually, one routine at a time. Then start all over again, because within a few weeks yet another habit will have formed and you will again start to lose focus and lapse into downtime.

The habit of breaking habits

Get into the habit of breaking habits. Move some furniture around. It will feel like working in another home or office and you might get some fresh ideas. This can be useful when the competition is strong and you are stuck for innovative ways of doing things. Question why you do things. Ask yourself why you:

◆ Write letters rather than telephone or fax (or vice versa)?
◆ Do some jobs weekly rather than daily, or monthly?
◆ Visit a client in person, rather than use some other form of communication?
◆ Operate an open door policy, which guarantees loss of control of time?
◆ Do certain jobs at all?

This is not so much about variety, or even change, as about creativity and ingenuity. It's about being smarter rather than quicker, or more efficient or popular. Most importantly, it's about being outcome- rather than task-oriented.

Creating quality downtime

It is just as important to have plenty of downtime as it is uptime, although for very different purposes. Downtime is when the creative right-brain can do its work and present its findings in the form of an idea, a new angle on a problem, or a 'eureka'. Unlike uptime, you can't assign downtime to specific tasks. You can't be sure that your mind will not move on to another subject, which 'it' (your subconscious guardian) perhaps considers more important for your welfare. An exception may be when you concentrate on a subject before going to sleep, and the answer arrives the following morning or during that day. The uptime thought is, in effect, handed over to your unconscious mind, for downtime (in this case sleep) processing.

There is no guarantee of this happening though. The downtime of a train journey might well cover a major problem you were struggling with before setting off, but don't depend on it. It might 'decide' to process completely different topics. So downtime planning is more to do with lifestyle and attitude – self-management – than task management. Significantly, based upon all our research, the biggest impact on output and project success comes from these periods of downtime.

Here is a very different exercise to ensure that quality thinking time is not squeezed out of your life.

Try it now   List any times that you are free to think in downtime. These will tend to be:

◆ When you are on your own.
◆ When you are unlikely to be interrupted – even for a short period, say when driving home.
◆ When whatever you are doing can be done without thinking – such as showering, getting dressed, knitting, or jogging.
◆ When you are relaxed.
◆ When you have to fill time – such as when waiting or travelling.
◆ When you are enjoying whatever you are doing – like gardening, washing the car, or having a hot bath.
◆ Just before going to sleep.

◆ Just after waking up.
◆ At work outside normal hours.

Think particularly of ways you can create more downtime. Don't encroach on the times you need for high concentration, or choose a time when other people are involved. Times when you are delayed, or waiting (say for a client, or a train) can be very productive downtime. Or consider starting a hobby involving an 'autopilot' skill which allows plenty of pleasurable, free thinking time.

Improving downtime quality

Think also of ways you can improve the *quality* of your downtimes, such as by:

◆ Making them more pleasurable (perhaps a scenic route rather than the motorway).
◆ Making them more private (switching off the telephone, locking your door, locating anonymously – such as in a hotel lounge).
◆ Timing them to fit your personal low concentration periods – keep to your personal 'clock'.
◆ Creating habits and associations (special places, chairs, walks).

Have a notebook or some system so that you do not forget ideas that come to you.

Daily practice

Another way to develop the ability to gain and maintain focus is to start an activity that involves practice every day. Regular practice forms empowering habits, which direct our behaviour unconsciously and optimise time. A new daily activity sounds like using up more time, but it need not. You are likely to have outcomes listed that happen to require regular practice, such as learning a language, playing a musical instrument, sketching, or learning a sport.

> Remember when you learned to drive a car. You had to maintain very high concentration – there was little chance of slipping into a daydream. This applies when learning any new skill until it becomes second nature.

So by choosing an outcome that really motivates you, you will fulfil a goal and at the same time get practice at staying in high focus. The secret is to practise every day. Once the habit is formed it becomes harder not to do the activity than to do it – even an initially hard task like running, or having a cold bath. This will require discipline, even if you enjoy the activity, as any new behaviour involves disruption and change. But the discipline of both making the time and staying alert is a transferable skill.

Some people seem able to move easily from one skill or interest to another, acquiring new knowledge and competence as they do. This gets easier with practice, as the same sort of skill is needed in each new situation. Top achievers have learned to concentrate fully whenever they need to, but also to cultivate important personal thinking time. Success, of course, breeds success. There is nothing better than a few achievements under your belt to boost your self-image as an achiever. Just follow some simple rules.

Daily practice rules

- Keep to any routine you decide upon.
- Preferably keep to the same time of the day and place.
- Keep your attention off other thoughts and distractions. Distractions will be less of a problem after a few sessions, so stay very aware at first.
- Don't take on too much each time, so that you don't get downhearted about progress.
- Learn one aspect – however minor – of your new skill at each session.
- Don't let your attention wander to your outcome – what it will be like to be a master at the activity. You can mentally rehearse your outcome the night before, perhaps.
- Confine your right-brain visualisation to downtime periods. Your immediate goal is to keep focused on what you are

doing at the moment.

◆ Watch out for tension in your body. New challenges can create tension, yet you will invariably do better in a skill when relaxed. The skill of being able to relax when in action is valuable, particularly when under time pressure.

◆ Use whatever relaxation techniques work for you.

Observation skills

Another way to help focus is to develop an interest involving careful observation. As we saw, it helps to change your routines. Some hobbies, such as photography, astronomy, sketching and painting, demand strong powers of observation. Like all skills, these come with practice. Here are some more ideas for improving your observation skills:

◆ Watch body language and non-verbal communication. There is so much to take in that you may have to restrict your observation to different aspects each day – tone of voice, emphasis on words, use of hands, eye movements, facial expression, stance and posture, sensory preference.

◆ Note how other people are motivated. Do they avoid unpleasantness, or move more positively towards pleasure? Do they need 'stroking' or can they motivate themselves internally? Is there a time of the day when you can expect more from a particular colleague?

◆ Watch a person who achieves a lot and manages their time well, and notice what they do.

◆ Expect to receive good ideas about your goals from everyday experiences – newspapers you read, conversations you overhear, things you see from the bus or train, features on the radio or television.

During a period when I did watercolour painting I got into the habit of viewing almost any suitable scene as if it were a painting, even mentally deciding on pigments and brushstrokes. Besides being helpful as mental practice, thus speeding up learning the skills, it enabled me to see almost everything around in a new light. A watery sky, for instance, took on special meaning for the first time. Another interest was sign writing such as seen on old shops – again opening up a new world using the powers of observation we all have. Many people are familiar with the skill of observation in their job or hobby. It is associated with pleasure and also with fast learning. It is also linked with quality uptime and the effective use of time.

Being more observant improves your control over yourself and what you do. Practise the important skill of moving into uptime, and staying there to accomplish what you set out to (to clear off a report, reorganise the garage, or learn a language) within a timescale. Once you have the skills, you are then free to make the choice between being in uptime or downtime, in high or low focus. That's when time mastery really happens and you surprise even yourself with what you achieve.

Focus and the thinking spectrum

The idea of focus is central to the so-called spectrum theory of thinking. We sometimes think about the brain functioning either in a logical, rational way, or in a creative, holistic mode. Alternatively, we think about conscious as opposed to unconscious thought. These are *either/or* ways of looking at thought. The spectrum theory, however (see Figure 15), sees thought as a *continuum*, ranging from very high focus (of the sort I have just described) to very low focus, as in sleep. Much of the time, when in conscious thought, we are well up the focus continuum. At other times, we are at the low focus, or downtime end associated with daydreaming, and letting the mind wander.

We move up and down this continuous spectrum constantly throughout the day. A long period of low focus can be interspersed with moments of very high focus, triggered by answering the doorbell, a telephone call, or being aware of brake lights on the motorway. Conversely, a period of high focus can be interrupted by a mental lapse, as our mind wanders, or we creatively explore some aspect of a problem. But we are never at both ends of the spectrum at the same time.

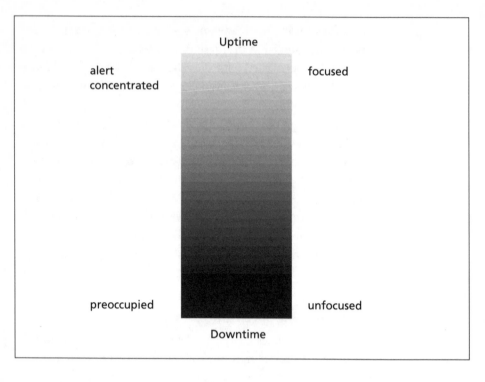

Fig. 15. The thinking spectrum.

Concepts or feelings

Besides being a useful way to think about thinking, the
thinking spectrum model has other significance.

- High focus is linked with abstract, conceptual thought and
  generalisations.
- Low focus thought is associated with concrete, subjective
  thought.

At a high level we might think about, say, a tree, using all our
'hard disk' memories of trees. It's like piling transparencies of
many trees on top of each other so that a single, common
shape, or concept, 'tree', comes into focus. At a low focus level
we might think about the tree at the end of the garden at our
favourite aunt's – a single, specific tree. Thence perhaps to
another tree, then by association to other concrete thoughts to
do with our aunt or other aspects of the memory. Here our

thoughts move laterally, as if from one transparency to another, rather than down a 'column' of like memories.

In each case, like thoughts attract like.

◆ In high focus mode the likeness is of concepts (like tree, green, or lonely).
◆ At low focus the likeness is feelings – the feeling evoked by the tree at the end of the garden, and the feeling that feeling in turn evoked.

In each case we are thinking, accessing memories and doing something with them. We could not have understood the concept of tree without the ability to focus back on lots of trees, but nor could we recall a feeling without some memory that triggered a similar emotion. Each has its place. Together, these produce the richness of the conscious mind.

Seeing a very old friend after many years we might be hard pressed to remember their name, or indeed anything about them. But in low focus – ideally below conscious level, when thinking about something else – the feelings evoked by the image of the face will make associations. In due course these will link with places and perhaps events, as well as the context of the memory, be it social or at work. The name will naturally emerge as part of our unconscious search. We may quickly register overall feelings – 'seeing' an intimidating schoolteacher might evoke feelings of fear, for example, long before we can give the feeling an explanation.

> We can choose where along the thinking spectrum we operate, depending on what we want to achieve.

One moment we conceptualise or rationalise. The next moment we call on intuitive feelings. Both 'brains' are serving us.

Each way of thinking affects our use of time. We have already seen how we need periods of high focus time to concentrate on specific tasks, but we have also seen how imaginative right-brain insights can dramatically increase our performance.

Moving up and down the thinking spectrum

Top time managers move freely up and down the focus spectrum. There are occasions when we need to get into top focus, and there are others when we need to let our feelings play a part, drawing on what would otherwise remain unconscious. So-called gut feelings, or intuitions, are an integral part of our total thinking. Because they are drawn from the subconscious, like dreams, they have an element of frankness and truth that does not always apply in high-level thought, when we can sometimes make excuses or kid ourselves. Having started with your logical 'list', priority ranking of both your outcomes and use of time calls for downtime creative thinking powers.

> In making important time decisions we need to move up and down the thinking spectrum.

Conscious planning is high focus, as is evaluating pros and cons in a critical, logical way. Getting insights about the validity of assumptions, judging the reliability of our information, or whether we can trust the people involved, demands more holistic, low focus skills. This is when we have to 'feel right' about something or someone.

Thinking par excellence: succeeding without trying

Some of our really clever analysis takes place in downtime. A brilliant insight might emerge at the surface of consciousness, of greater quality than weeks of arduous analysis. This is low-focus thinking par excellence – succeeding without trying. This is where the most successful users of time seem to have the edge. They steer through the trickiest problems with apparent ease and confidence. They know what it is to 'feel right' about something. That's what gives them the motivation to get on with the task rather than procrastinate. They have been given the green light from below the limited threshold of conscious thought. All this is primarily right-brain, downtime processing. It doesn't happen to workaholics, who excel in inputs rather than outputs.

For example, one chief executive described how he had a

major report to write, with major implications for his company. He struggled over it for several weeks. Then in the small hours of one Saturday morning he awoke with the solution ready made, and proceeded to write the long report. By midday on the Saturday a complete and final report was finished, addressing all the thorny issues involved as though he had been helped by some outside divine consultant. That's the power of right-brain thinking, and it does things for your time management that no known 'system' can ever do. Yet it's a universal human skill that can be fostered and fully harnessed.

Others are familiar with the experience of waking in the morning and discovering to their delight that big problems of the night before have all but vanished in the light of a new day. Sometimes such insights come when shaving, showering or driving to the office (all 'low spectrum' for most people). The same principle applies: the harder you try, the worse the results.

> Your sophisticated brain has to be harnessed and not commandeered.

Creative insights are more likely to completely remove a problem than just save you ten per cent of your time in tackling it. This is the smart way of using your brain, and it happens at the low focus end of the spectrum. Interspersed with high-focus periods, and matched with priority outcomes, you can use the thinking spectrum to get what is most important to you.

CHAPTER 11

Insight, Incubation and Creativity

Sleeping on a problem has well-proven benefits and can enhance creativity and improve the quality of your decisions.

S leeping on a problem is a familiar concept. The times when we use it, however, are all too rare compared with the times we adopt a conscious thinking mode when tackling day-to-day problems. Typically, the incubation mode of thinking occurs by default. We are overwhelmed by a problem and can do nothing but either put it out of mind, because some other issue takes over, or literally 'sleep on it' – leaving it until the following day. Often by the following morning things do not seem quite as bad as they were, or we have a couple of ideas we can work on that might help. In some cases the problem has all but evaporated.

This is not a matter of chance. It is the highly effective but unconscious thought processing stage we term *incubation*. This chapter applies this and other aspects of our thinking to a familiar model of the stages of thinking. The model can be applied to any problem or project, and particularly applies when we want to make the most of our time. An holistic thinking approach which produces significant rather than marginal improvements can be achieved. That means you can double and treble your output. This applies even in the case of tasks and responsibilities in respect of which we can boast plenty of skill and experience.

A better way of thinking

There are certain attractions to this 'subterranean' way of thinking for time-challenged executives.

Cleverer than conscious thinking

According to the top executives I met as part of leadership research, logical thought processes are often enhanced by intuition, 'sleeping on a problem', or just 'a good idea' that came from nowhere. One way or another, they finished up with a better solution. Sometimes we have difficulty working a great idea backwards, to show its reasoning, even though it is patently 'right'. Similarly, we may have difficulty in communicating the idea to others, especially the details of implementation. But the insight or idea itself is of weightier mental stuff. We often struggle to fully understand a solution that is particularly original, let alone express it in sequential steps – 'did I think of that?' The idea comes 'ready made'. Somehow logical stages are leapfrogged, yet the outcome equals or betters painstaking research and analysis.

Our modern, technologically driven society has come about through a long succession of imaginative advances that each took us a big leap forward. We cannot compete with the computer in terms of sequential logic or number crunching, but the human imagination occupies a very different dimension. No problem is too difficult if we are willing to 'let go' and sleep on it.

Brain without pain

Thought incubation happens at the same time as you are doing other useful things, like driving to the office, having a shower, or sleeping. Into the bargain, you do what you do in the best way, achieving the best solutions.

It is closely related to relaxation and harmony with the body. It doesn't produce the stress of other techniques that require a lot of effort for little gain. We actually seem to thrive on insights, eurekas and intuitive thought. This is the enjoyable, user-friendly side of thought processing. It's brainwork that doesn't hurt.

Getting incubation in context

Having given some recognition to this somewhat mystical aspect of our thinking, let's consider the stages of thinking we usually go through when solving a problem or making a decision. Some of these thinking stages are usually applied to formal project management or problem-solving. I use them here to illustrate the way the left- and right-sides of the brain come into play when solving time management or any other problems. The model illustrates how some aspects of the process, like incubation, can easily be undervalued.

Thinking stages

Think of actual tasks or problems that take up your time as you consider these stages, and which side of the brain is being called upon.

1. **Preparation.** This is the planning stage, at which we gather data, state the problem clearly and make any assumptions. It is where goal setting happens and outcomes are set. You get your direction right, check on your resources and think ahead. All the tests of a good outcome that we covered in Chapter 3 are part of your preparation in solving your 'outcome problem' – the problem of how to get to B (your outcome) when you are at A.

2. **Frustration.** This stage is conspicuously missing from many problem-solving models, and rarely figures in super time management systems, but most of us are all too familiar with it. It might involve feeling bored, despondent or irritable. It is associated with coming up against brick walls, wondering whether you will ever see the light at the end of the tunnel, or not being able to see the wood for the trees. Sometimes we simply get stuck. This stage is often accompanied by a feeling of inadequacy, and doubt as to whether a solution exists at all.

3. **Incubation.** As we have already seen, sometimes we stop trying, put the matter on hold and forget about it for a while. This might be because we are stuck. More often, our minds become occupied with another matter, perhaps a new priority. Either way, the problem goes below the surface. It might be for moment, for a night, or even for weeks.

4. **Insight.** Then comes the inspiration. This might be when you least expect it, probably when you are in a relaxed mood, doing something quite distinct from your problem solving. Sometimes you are just a spectator as the solution, or at least a positive lead forward, comes out of the blue.

Even minor revelations are welcome and pleasant, and most of us wish they would come more often. The whole phenomenon, however, can be missing from a professional or textbook way of addressing problems. It is not consistent, so it seems, with achieving tight deadlines in high-focus thinking mode, and staying in control of your time and thought. It is too imprecise, too unreliable and too mystical. You feel you have got to *do* something to solve your problem. But when this stage is bypassed, because of time pressure, or when an insight is suppressed or rejected out of hand, priceless, timesaving ideas may be lost in the name of reason.

5. **Working out**. Finally you have to check out your insights, get them into some suitable form and turn them into reality. This is the working-out or implementation stage. You have to be pragmatic and rational, and ensure you achieve hard results. You have to put your plans into practice, and achieve 'bottom line' results.

Try it now

From what you have learnt so far about how the brain works, consider which thinking modes apply to these thinking stages. Make a cross on the continuum between left and right for each stage. A strongly logical, analytical, or high focus thought process would fall well to the left. Creative, imaginative, intuitive thought – or downtime mode – would be over to the right. If you consider a mixture of thinking is involved, put a mark somewhere in between.

	Left brain	**Right brain**
Preparation		
Frustration		
Incubation		
Insight		
Working out		

A universal model

This problem-solving model is remarkably consistent in its application to all kinds of problems. In particular it applies on any timescale, and whatever the size of the problem, project or problem being addressed. The planning part of writing a letter or making a telephone call is just as important in its context as the planning phase of a major corporate project lasting months. The incubation stage can be very short, although you might not be conscious of it in the way you are when sitting down to sort out your problem or work out the implementation of a solution. Incubation can happen any time after the issue, outcome, or problem has been 'registered' with the subconscious. As we saw earlier, it can last from moments to literally years.

Thinking like two people

From stage to stage you operate like two different people, one thinking consciously, logically and analytically, the other in an imaginative but more passive mode. Two minds are at work. Separately they might well produce only mediocrity – logical solutions that any rational competitor might think of, or alternatively brilliant ideas that never see the light of day. Together, however, the left and right brain can be a formidable duo, making the impossible possible.

Creativity at every stage

The time management secret is to inject creativity into every part of the thinking process so that it affects your attitude and very way of life. In particular you need to be more aware of the unconscious processes so that you can foster them in everyday situations. During the rest of this chapter we shall see how the right brain plays its part at every stage, and what you can do to make your overall thinking more effective.

Preparing for success

Let's apply some right-brain thought to the preparation stage. This is usually thought of as a left-brain, high-focus function (how did you allocate it on the left-brain/right-brain axis?). The same applies to the later implementation stage, usually associated with hands-on action rather than creative thought. I will give a lot of attention therefore to the preparation and planning stage to illustrate the scope for creativity and unconscious processing.

Planning usually involves making certain logical assumptions upon which the success of our task will depend, but if these assumptions are to be valid they need to be questioned by insightful, creative thinking. This may well save lots of unnecessary time and effort. If the subject is a familiar one, because it is your business, your job, or your industry, there is a danger that assumptions will be no better than pattern-based mindsets. The process of seeing things from a new perspective, of seeing the big picture, of turning things on their head, is not one we can do by greater focus, or further analysis of familiar mental patterns. It sometimes requires the naivety of someone who is not familiar with the subject or problem, who can ask penetrating questions. Or use your own, holistic brain.

What about the data upon which assumptions are based?

◆ Where did this come from?
◆ Who says so?
◆ Do we need more data?
◆ How significant might the missing data be?
◆ Is there time to get more?
◆ Do we make the best of what we have got?
◆ Which data are the most critical?

These are judgements, and by their nature judgements are not amenable to sequential, logical techniques. But nor are they beyond the wit of the most harassed, time-pressured person. The vital factor to a successful outcome may be a simple, naive question – a new angle on an all-too-familiar problem. This process is intuitive rather than cerebral. As we have seen you are as likely to get an insight when showering, driving to work, or at 3am as in a meeting or during planned thinking time in the office. And that can transform a sterile, two-dimensional plan, and prepare you for a successful outcome.

Creative problem definition

In the right frame of mind, and given the 'space' of an appropriate lifestyle, problems can be *creatively redefined*. In such a way the problem:

◆ becomes clearer
◆ disappears altogether
◆ or better still is turned into a positive opportunity.

Hours and days of time can be created as you think differently about your outcomes and how to achieve them. That is radical time management.

There are plenty of techniques to help you generate new ideas, or perhaps stimulate your right-brain, some of which are explained in the final chapter, but you can start with the principles already outlined. Think in terms of outcomes – what are you after, where are you going? Remember the tests we applied in Chapter 3. Think also in terms of outputs – what you get out rather than what you put in. Think in terms of:

◆ results rather than frantic activity or clever systems
◆ your time as an investment, and the return it can give you.

Most of all, start to trust your own amazing creative powers.

Planning with mental images

Another right-brain aspect concerns the way outcomes are fixed clearly in your mind. We know the importance of writing down goals, defining the problem, and focusing on the facts and figures of your goal. But we have also seen the power of creating your outcome as an internal sensory experience. For the individual (companies don't have this skill; they don't even have brains, just Articles of Association), strong visualisation translates the outcome into a target. This creates the sophisticated subconscious associations that provide the day-to-day ideas and insights that bring about success.

Vividly imagined goals are more powerful than words or abstractions. They are experiences that, as far as the brain is concerned, have *happened*. It follows that if something has happened, it must be *possible*.

> Research has shown that what we believe to be possible has a high chance of success.

Technically, by mental rehearsal, we can 'see it happening'. Your mind then has a blueprint that it adheres to relentlessly until your goal is achieved – until subjective reality is turned into objective reality. New desires and mental images then take over, with new outcomes. This helps to explain what we hear about the power of vision, or a personal dream.

People with vision

All this is hard for the left-brain corporate animal to digest. Corporations have their plans, of course, and there are some links between the ways we work out problems and how we structure problem-solving or goal-achievement in an organisation. But people, not organisations, have dreams and visions, hopes and desires. People, not structures or systems, make decisions. A legal entity does not get flashes of inspiration. The nearest it has to a brain is the systems-based analytical clone of the human left-brain we know as a bureaucracy. There is a pathetic symbiosis between bureaucratic organisations and the left-brain managers who perpetuate them. Thinking is done by people. A corporate bureaucracy or super computer cannot replace the imaginative, creative part of that thinking.

Bringing a written plan to life

You cannot give too much attention to the preparation stage. How you spend much of your time will be determined at this stage. If you miss it out, your time is still spoken for. But in some random way that may have nothing to do with your real outcomes, which will inevitably create the bottlenecks and stresses for which 'time' is usually blamed. However, you can bring a written plan to life by incorporating right-brain imagery or mental rehearsal. You can get to know the *language* of the right brain – senses rather than symbols – and use it to communicate with your most creative, productive 'self'.

Reconciling your two minds

The frustration stage confirms the inadequacy of following a logical process. Doubts about whether there really is a solution to whatever we are faced with are bound to arise, but frustration is on your side in the time battle. It is part of the conflict between logic and feeling, heart and mind. It's a cue that saves rather than costs time. At some point we have to reconcile our 'two minds' and come up with what is best. Once you have made your mind up things usually get easier, even though there may be many hurdles still to overcome. Frustration can be the trigger that calls on the subconscious to come up with the goods. So it can be a critical stage, even though often resented and viewed as a drain on time and energy.

Many educationalists and professional managers confuse this important stage with muddy thinking or indecision. In fact it is a signal to stop trying too hard, and to let your whole brain do the work. It means it is time to think about or do something else, to take your mind off the immediate problem. It might mean changing your attitude.

> Used positively, frustration can bring about a break-through to a higher level of thinking – perhaps a completely new angle on the problem.

This is the time to switch tasks, clean out the cupboard or garage, have a game of squash or go for a walk with the dog. Or maybe do nothing – just sleep on it.

Mentally lying down

Incubating your thoughts is a central feature of quality thinking. If you don't make arrangements for it to happen by your attitude and lifestyle, your subconscious 'master controller' will take over and ensure that for your own welfare you literally sleep on the matter. This is a compulsory phenomenon, including dreaming, which sensibly does what the conscious but limited mind cannot provide for. So the worst results of restricting your thinking to the visible part of the mental iceberg are avoided naturally.

Downtime involves more than just sleep however. You can't stop ideas coming the following day if they decide to. You can't stop your mind wandering during an important meeting and seeing another point of view, or thinking about something more useful to your outcomes – of higher priority. And you can't help feeling that something, or somebody, is right or wrong, even though you don't know why. What you can do, however, is quickly suppress such thoughts, rationalise them away, or simply not trust them without the chapter and verse of conscious, sequential reasoning. Faced with such ungrateful habits of attitude and belief, it is not surprising that our creative mental powers atrophy like an arm continuously tied in a sling. Identifying and correcting these habits is the radical but effective way to managing your time and life.

Ideas from outside

The insight stage is the one we usually associate with creative thinking. These moments can change a whole situation round in an instant. They can produce the most complete, detailed solutions, including 'blueprints' for implementation.

How to do a task in one quarter of the time it has taken in the past is more likely to come through this thinking route than through further analysis or a consultancy assignment. The more such creative 'experiences' you can capture, the better. Go for quantity initially. Quality will come in due course as you trust your insight in more and more areas of your life, and build up your mental databank through wider interests and personal associations. Most importantly, allow your creative self-trust to extend to every stage of the thinking process, and to any place, time or situation. Don't allow your right-brain to be locked-out or suppressed.

Creativity and the bottom line

Unlike the eureka stage, the implementation stage is not usually thought of as the creative part of a project or task. This again illustrates blinkered thinking. The infinite possibilities of a holistic solution are replaced by a finite agenda or analysis. Typically the emphasis is on doing without thinking rather than thinking and doing. This is very prevalent in a hands-on, short-term results culture. Holistic thinkers never stop looking for choices. They never stop believing there is a better way, and this carries on right through the implementation phase. Facing any sort of competition, you dare not stop being creative.

Creativity is not just about blue-sky research or the new wonder product. For instance, it might result in an efficiency improvement that makes a critical cost difference, or that allows faster turnaround of a product or service. It might involve new processes and materials, new places or people. It will affect outputs and the bottom line.

> You don't stop planning; you don't stop incubating. You expect more and better insights each day.

Each implementation problem, whether intractable or seemingly simple, forms a new cycle in the thinking process, with more planning, frustration, incubation and – thankfully – insights.

This is how individuals and companies become innovative. It happens by a change in individual thinking and belief, rather than because of new reporting lines or a mission statement. Corporately it has to start at the top, where culture is set and role models tend to be established. Some companies give special attention to innovation in certain pockets of the business, such as new product development or identifying new markets. But true creative thinking rarely penetrates the black hole of administration and overhead. Nor is it a feature of professional managers in the way they plan and use their time. Releasing your right-brain powers, changing your attitudes, breaking up familiar patterns of thinking and behaviour is the way to solve the problem of 'time'.

Now go back and see whether you want to amend your left-brain/right-brain positioning at the beginning of the chapter. None of what we have discussed devalues the role of analytical thought, provided it is complemented with a holistic, creative perspective. That is the way of two-sided, bicameral thinking and the secret of top time managers.

CHAPTER 12

Getting More Brainpower

T he human brain thinks in different ways at the same time. The left-brain tends to see things as constituent parts, each having to be identified, understood and analysed in an attempt to make sense of the whole. This is the basis of conscious thought. Any major task or project is thought out in this analytical way, which is seen in the standard 'planning, control, monitoring and evaluation' we associate with any management activity. When making a decision we might list the pros and cons, then perhaps further break down and analyse each item. A tricky problem is also broken down into bits we can manage. Left-brain thinking also accounts for the predominance of analytical approaches to time management.

The right-brain, on the other hand, thinks holistically, seeing things as a whole. We speak of 'getting things in perspective', or 'seeing the big picture'. This form of thought processing is done in parallel, rather than in sequence. We cannot think of several things at once in a highly conscious way, but multi-processing is carried out in the unconscious part of our mind – what is often described as the submerged part of the mental iceberg. Experts say that more than 90 per cent of all our mental processes are in this unconscious category.

The differences are fundamental. So much so that the best thinkers frequently have a dilemma, as they are confronted with different 'conclusions' – 'I'm in two minds about this.' One 'conclusion' is likely to be based on cool, hard logic. The other will reflect feelings or intuition, characteristic of the lower end of the focus spectrum, subconscious thought and the right-brain. The latter, although not always supported (initially at least) by left-brain rationale, tends to influence decisions strongly in some people, but less so in others. Top business leaders, for instance, tend to value and use intuition highly, in all sorts of ways, not least in making the most of their time. This occurs, however, as a complement to logical analysis, and neither form of thought predominates. It also involves flexibility and variety in the way we think and live, which are covered in this chapter.

Flexible thinking

One of the weaknesses of left-brain thinking is its inflexibility. It tends to follow a sequential, rigid course until a plausible solution is found. This may not, however, be the best solution. Unidentified alternatives at each stage in the process, by their nature, are excluded. Indeed, without processing in parallel, or in effect repeating the relatively inefficient sequential operation an infinite number of times, there is no chance of optimal solutions being uncovered. So if we are determined to confine our data gathering and processing to the visible part of the brain iceberg, we can be no better than mediocre. Mediocrity will then be displayed in the way we use our time, and in turn what we achieve.

Sequential and parallel thinking

Let me illustrate this inflexibility, and the different ways of thinking on which it is based, with a simple exercise. The exercise involves arranging simple shapes to form another shape that can be easily described.

Two plastic or cardboard shapes, 1 and 2 are offered, and the 'solution' is usually a square, as shown in Figure 16. Another shape (3) is then offered, and this is usually added to the square to form a rectangle. Two further shapes are then offered, 4 and 5, which can eventually be made to create another square. A sixth shape is offered, and this seems to present an insoluble problem.

A different way of arranging the shapes is shown in Figure 17. The solution is not complex, and is perfectly logical – with hindsight, which is characteristic of holistic thinking. It is also simple, another feature of the best solutions. More important, however, and also characteristic of right-brain thinking, it turns out to be *better* than the best solution based on sequential processing. The second arrangement, however, is less likely to be tried, and the reasons are related to the dominant, left-brain way

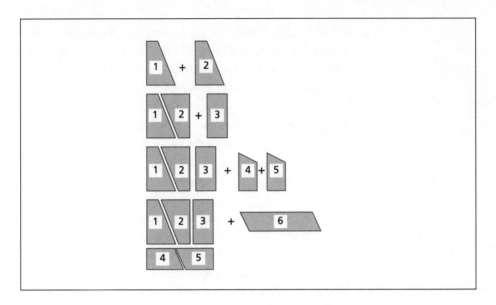

Fig. 16. Left-brain sequential thinking.

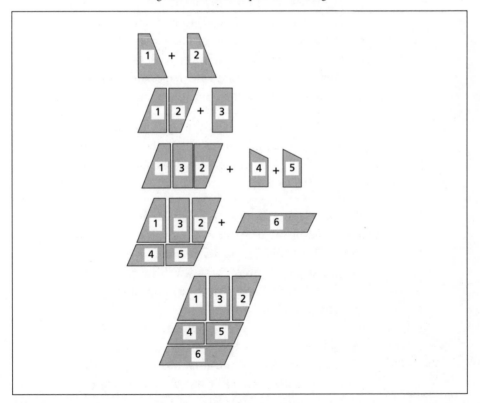

Fig. 17. Right-brain parallel thinking.

of thinking I have described. Such linear processing is the norm, and almost any problem-solving skill training will reflect this – the illustration gives us clues about how we can adopt a more flexible, successful approach to problems.

Why does the exercise present any difficulty? Maybe the parallelogram is not as obvious as a square, so was not adopted at the first stage, but this is not an adequate answer. There is no reason why any answer should be the most obvious one. Surely this is what we find in everyday life.

Once started off, the shapes would have had to be rearranged in order to proceed. So even if each stage is correct, or feasible, the problem has to be restated and tackled all over again as new data emerge. As well as being keen on the familiar square (the brain likes to deal in familiar concepts and patterns), it is unlikely that we will want to undo an earlier solution in the light of new inputs.

As we saw in an earlier chapter, the tendency of the brain to create patterns and stick to them is strong. In everyday situations we tend to reinforce our earlier actions, justifying them, or making 'excuses'. So we overlook the new circumstances (in this case new shapes are presented), and miss opportunities that are there for the taking.

> Left-brain thinking tends to go for the first feasible solution, as though there were only one solution so this must be it. In the complexity of real life this tendency does not serve us well.

You will also see that the solutions that were adopted were influenced by the order in which data arrived. Again, in real life, we don't have the luxury of ordering the many circumstances and events with which we have to deal. They just happen and this makes a rigid planning approach to time management all but useless. The only thing we can be certain of is uncertainty and change. One new 'shape' can scupper the best-laid plan.

Creative thinking is in constant battle with this tendency to build on existing, convenient thought patterns to reach plausible solutions. Using the brain landscape analogy, we take the easy or natural course and follow the contours of a familiar landscape.

Our logical, cerebral thinking purports to address a problem objectively and to consider all available data. Ironically, however, it is as blinkered and naive as it is subjective. We each have different mental patterns, which we almost blindly adhere to.

Losing control by trying too hard

It can be frustrating to have to adopt a different way of thinking. We don't like change. Parallel thinking is largely done, as we have seen, below our consciousness, so it seems we are no longer masters of the problem-solving process. Holistic thinking does not happen in high-focus uptime. Such focused thinking is vertical, rather than horizontal or parallel ('lateral thinking', as Edward de Bono coined the term). It deals with *parts* rather than the whole. Its raw material is concepts rather than concrete reality. Nor does parallel thinking sit comfortably with the modern, action-oriented executive who likes to apply energy and inputs – to do something visible.

> As well as the personal frustration and change that is involved, there are cultural and organisational barriers to creative thinking.

One trainer used an interesting device to help trainees get into the relaxed mode that is associated with creativity. Delegates were wired up to an electric train-set in a way that set the train running when they recorded low brain cycle alpha waves. The usual rules were reversed, and the harder executives tried, the less they were able to make the train move. Those who relaxed, or were not naturally competitive, soon had the train whizzing round the track. This illustrates the frustration involved in harnessing non-conscious parts of our thinking. It fits well with the time-proven truism, 'The harder I try the worse I get.'

More parallel thinking

Each time management issue is a problem, or can be restated as one, but classical problem-solving techniques follow distinctly left-brain thinking processes. We can start to apply more parallel thinking, however, and thus generate more options, and better solutions, in holistic mode. In real life problems involving people and precious time, we are not dealing with single solutions or black-or-white absolutes. Another shape – another variable – can change the whole situation. And it usually does. Many of these new shapes are there all along – we just don't bother to look for them. So the 'sensory acuity' I talked about earlier is an important skill. We need to be aware of what is going on.

Thankfully, the billions of external sensual stimuli don't all need to pass through our conscious understanding, although they play their part below the surface. A rich environment will provide rich data. We can decide who and what we associate with that will provide the rich mental databank upon which quality thought is based. Variety of environment promotes this flexibility of thought. In the final chapter on reframing I describe specific techniques to generate alternatives, and thus better solutions.

Getting more from your right-brain

Switching from sequential to parallel thinking mode will have a big effect on how you use your time. Solutions arrived at by ordinary, conscious thinking processes tend to be incremental at best, and often the law of diminishing returns applies – you get less and less from your effort. In some cases we seem to go backwards. Time spent fruitlessly creates other time bottlenecks and new problems. An even greater negative effect can result from the inherent added guilt and inevitable blow to our self-image.

This explains the relative ineffectiveness of conventional time management theory, biased as it is towards left-brain problem-solving methods. The surprising insights of holistic solutions, however, typically result in extraordinary changes in both outlook and behaviour. As old patterns are demolished there is room for completely new perspectives. Problems are restated, scenarios are recreated and constraints are removed. So, for example, some tasks might be eliminated altogether with a holistic view, not just of the problem, but also of the outcomes in mind and the different ways to achieve those outcomes. This defies credibility in hardened left-brain executives. However, a few truly excellent people move from success to success, using the same brain hardware as their mediocre colleagues. Rather than depend on systems, structures and other pattern-based thinking, the creative time manager harnesses the other latent side of his or her standard-issue brain.

Practical benefits

This results in all sorts of practical benefits. For example:

◆ When driving to work your mind seems to decide on which are the most important tasks to clear, and at the same time you mentally rehearse the telephone calls and personal meetings that are necessary. It turns out that you achieve a lot more than usual that day.

◆ When relaxing at the weekend, a difficult task you have been struggling over suddenly seems to do itself, taking a fraction of the time it would normally take.

◆ A simple idea that 'came from nowhere' results in a solution to a personal relationship problem.

◆ The choice of who will form a special project team at work comes to you when watching your children playing in the park, and turns out to be critical to the success of the project. The 'solution' came as a surprise even to you, but with hindsight it made good sense.

◆ By visualising different scenarios ahead for a reorganisation some factors crop up which would not be feasible, and which you had not thought of in all the planning meetings. Plans are changed and critical obstacles are avoided.

◆ You get an idea on how you can cut right down on telephone charges.

Trusting your mind resources

Such examples are common, and simply illustrate what might be happening below the conscious mind. Most of us could benefit from both scale and frequency of creative thinking. The big change starts when you learn to trust the staggering processing power you have at your disposal. To do this you will need to adopt an attitude, and if need be a lifestyle, that fosters rather than suppresses your insight and creativity. Self-image is central. The underlying self-image that says: 'I am capable of almost anything, there is no problem that I cannot face, I have no reason to short-change myself. . .' will achieve more than a whole portfolio of time management systems. Find examples of human excellence among your friends or colleagues, or those you admire from a distance. Watch busy, output-oriented people at work and voluntary organisations, achieving with ease what others will never achieve in a lifetime. You will notice a congruence of self-belief and behaviour, and a balance of heart and mind. Both sides of the brain are used.

Believing in yourself

The bicameral (two-sided) thinker is literally more balanced. He or she uses more brain resources, and this can show itself in greater confidence and self-esteem. Self-image, or any long-standing part of our personality, is just another way we structure our thought, but at a higher, 'macro' level. Self-image is self-perception, but still perception – a way of seeing things, or thinking. We follow habitual mental strategies, for better or worse, in pursuance of what we consider worthwhile intentions. These 'strategies' include self-beliefs. It is our way of getting what we want. This is to do with brain software, not hardware. Imagining, or visualising can change everything, including patterns of connections – feelings, beliefs and attitudes – however long-standing.

The brain is as amenable to exercises as a limb recovering from under-use following injury. And these thinking strategies control just about all of our waking lives. The bad news is that we don't take change lightly. The good news is that a newly created thinking strategy will bring about immediate and sometimes dramatic change in our behaviour and achievements. Incorporate imagination as well as rationale. Harness the unconscious part of your mind. Start addressing how you use your time from the master control room of your bicameral brain.

Try something different

Flexibility is an aspect of achievement that applies to far more than time management. Having observed what happens when we do something (using sensory acuity) we need to have the flexibility to try something different, and to keep on trying until we achieve the outcome we want. This is similar to a classical cybernetic or feedback system, in which negative feedback information is used to progressively move towards a target. Human beings, of course, are the supreme example of such a system. This is the system we harness when types of behaviour (besides life-serving outcomes such as respiration and pulse rate) become what we describe as 'unconscious competence'.

Used at a higher level, say in problem-solving or goal-achievement, the system works on the basis of trust. You need to trust your unconscious brain's ability to choose, from potentially countless sensual stimuli, those that will help you to achieve your desired goals. For example, a casual conversation or something you read in a magazine article can trigger a line of thought that results in an insight, a better way of doing things, or an important new angle on a situation or problem. This 'trusting' way draws on all your sensory experiences and links them with your outcomes by association. By tapping into the 'black box' of your own cybernetic goal-achieving system, you can tackle the most intractable time management problems without really trying.

Harnessing your built-in goal-achieving mechanism

The cybernetic system, however, cannot be used to order. It does not respond to tight deadlines, for instance ('I want a blinding flash by 5 o'clock please'). The first or most plausible answer is not automatically accepted. A true 'parallel search' is applied to each problem. So it will take as long as it takes. Nothing but the best will suffice.

As we saw at the start, if you have an important deadline, like going on holiday, the chances are you will achieve what you are determined to (your outcomes) in time, even though you are hardly aware of how you managed it. But in doing so you are calling on extra subconscious powers that normally go unused.

Taking control by losing control

Low-focus, right-brain thinking seems to be right outside our control. In fact a different sort of control is needed over right-brain thought processes. In the short term you seem to be at the mercy of a process you don't understand. But in the longer term you can start to take control of your habits, attitudes and way of life in such a way that you in fact have far greater control over what you want to do or be. The delegates wired up to the electric train-set took control when they *relinquished* control. They got what they wanted when they harnessed the right-side of their brain.

You may have to accept a level of flexibility and self-trust that you are uncomfortable with. But it is this very flexibility and self-trust that produces the seemingly random associations and options upon which the best solutions depend. The answer is inside, and the skill is to let it out.

Flexibility and feedback for success

Flexibility is also an essential part of a familiar four-step model of success.

1. Decide on your outcome.
2. Do what you think will bring it about.
3. Be alert and notice what you are achieving.
4. Have the flexibility to keep changing until you get your outcome.

This feedback mode depends on having a clear target or outcome, mechanisms to detect negative feedback – the extent to which you are missing your goal – and the ability and willingness to change direction as you receive feedback.

I have already stressed the importance of outcomes. Sensory acuity also keeps cropping up in time mastery. We must be able to recognise the results of our actions, or we will keep doing the same things and missing our target. But this feedback is internal as well as external. We have seen, for instance, the importance of feelings and intuition, and of listening to our inner voice.

Flexibility of thinking, as well as of behaviour, is needed. This is sometimes the hardest, as we are creatures of habit and resist change. Amazingly, we are more inclined to keep doing the same thing over and over again even when it has failed once or more. We keep trying harder, having the same attitude and beliefs, rather than make the changes that will increase our options, and consequently our chances of success.

Creating variety

Seeing things in a different way means flexibility of thinking and attitude, and some control over how we feel. Our level of motivation to do any task will determine how well we do it, and how long it takes us. Boredom not only reduces our effectiveness but it can cause stress even more than when we are over-stretched. Work involving little or no imagination is a killer. Conversely, when there is variety there can be a great sense of fulfilment and job satisfaction.

Recent developments in self-managing teams, where there is variety of work, show productivity increases, as well as higher morale. To handle a whole project, or make a complete product, for example, in the way a traditional craftsman would do, enhances job satisfaction when compared with doing even the most complicated part of the total project over and over again – but that is just what modern specialisation of labour demands. Variety is engineered out in the name of cost efficiency. By building in variety, however, the tasks themselves can become intrinsic rewards, and thus provide the necessary motivation. This is a fundamental feature of time effectiveness. As we saw, rewards do not have to be monetary, or even material. They can come from the simple satisfaction of doing a job well:

◆ a finished article
◆ a completed project
◆ or some visible, discrete outcome.

Simply by arranging your tasks so that you have plenty of variety, you will increase your output. A nasty little job will be got rid of quickly, as you mentally look towards something more enjoyable. A task involving a lot of high-focus concentration, in which your brain seems to grind, is best followed by something you can do 'with your eyes closed', leaving your mind to wander in low-focus downtime, dreaming about things you like to dream about. Then back to something more mentally taxing.

Introducing variety

As well as ranking tasks according to importance *vs* urgency, or tasteful *vs* distasteful, as we discussed earlier, you can introduce simple variety. This can be between high and low concentration as we saw in the previous chapter, or long jobs can be interspersed with a few very short ones. Depending on the work you do, sitting-down jobs can be interspersed with standing-up ones. Jobs involving getting outside your office and meeting other people can be placed between tasks that tie you to your office, and so on. It doesn't cost anything. It just means recognising the way you think and act instinctively. It means you are in control, and most of all it enhances your effectiveness and use of time.

Starting a new exercise book

You can introduce variety in other ways. You may be able to change your immediate working environment from time to time. It's hard to get into a rut when things around keep changing. Do you remember starting a new exercise book at school? For a while everything was super-neat and your motivation was high. Introducing variety is like punctuating your life with lots of clean new exercise books – lots of new starts.

This is an apparently disorganised way of working that appeals better to some people than others (probably those who got a high right-brain psychometric score). But it certainly helps creativity, as does any novelty. For people working from home, and those free to manage their working day, variety in when you do things can also keep you in top form, maintaining peak focus when you need it. You may not be aware of which times of the day are more productive for you, other than maybe first thing in the morning which is the case with most people. You can begin to experiment with 'prime time' management by changing some routines around. Figure 18 is based on a wide survey, but you can check your own daily

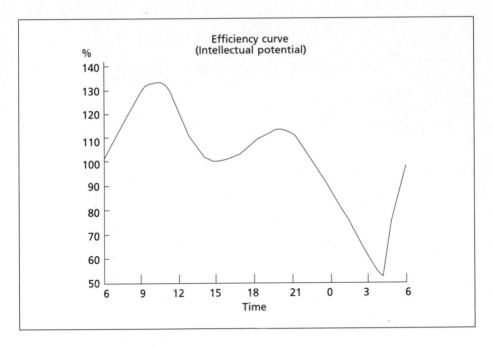

Fig. 18. Personal timing.

clock and build your schedule accordingly. This is another part of our behaviour that is master-minded below the conscious level, but that can become an ally with understanding and common sense.

Variety, as well as flexibility, is a major thinking requirement. We think in different ways for different purposes. This is illustrated by the thinking spectrum and also by the different thinking stages from the conception of an idea to its final realisation. Time management is all about achievement – producing outputs, or results. This demands quality thinking – in the broad sense we have discussed, which includes attitude and belief. You can become more flexible in your thinking by organising more quality downtime into your life, and calling on the lateral thinking power of the right brain. Changing your routines, as described in the previous chapter, will help to disturb some of the inflexible mindsets that prevent creativity. Introducing variety – even by reordering what you would do in any event – would create the important motivation and alertness that means better use of your time. All this adds up to better thinking.

CHAPTER 13

Creative Problem-Solving

'Reframing' – seeing something in a different light, or from a new perspective – is what creative thinking is all about. It involves breaking down familiar mental patterns that stop us seeing options and opportunities. Time itself can be reframed. The opportunity to spend five minutes with a world celebrity you have always admired, for example, puts an immediate high value on those few minutes. An extra five minutes in bed at the weekend, on the other hand, is framed very differently.

Depending on how we frame things, we will both feel and behave differently. This requires some creative thinking. By being able to imagine otherwise familiar situations in many and varied frames, we have a thinking tool that can be used in all sorts of positive ways.

This final chapter describes some reframing techniques that can be applied to time management and personal development, illustrating how they can help solve specific, time-related problems.

Sleight of mouth

Some of the responses to the Meta Model, referred to in Chapter 9, involve reframing. A 'universal quantifier' contains an absolute such as 'never', 'always', 'every' and so on. We frequently make statements such as 'I never . . .' or 'she always . . .' which a moment's thought (just based on the laws of probability) would quickly undermine. Questions like: 'Never? Are there no circumstances in which . . .?' respond challengingly to such unthinking language patterns. Essentially ubiquitous language such as generalisation demands deliberate, different perspectives if we are to get at their true meaning – if you like, what the speaker is really wanting to communicate.

Other techniques popular with NLP practitioners are also

useful for reframing. One, called *sleight of mouth* (alluding to the conjuror's sleight of hand) suggests patterns of response to what might be called a 'problem statement'. This is an exercise in generating new points of view, which is the essence of creative time management. It turns things on their head, sees them from another viewpoint, takes a counter position, looks on the bright side, looks on the dark side and so on. It is an important right-brain skill worth developing.

Each 'pattern' can open new angles of thinking on the problem. You will already be familiar with some of the approaches, such as taking a 'helicopter view', or breaking down the problem into smaller parts (including 'chunking' goals into smaller ones, that we have already met), trying to see a 'silver lining', turning a problem into an opportunity and so on. Using a common time management statement as an example – 'There's too much work to handle' – the various sleight of mouth perspectives and suggested responses are shown in Figure 19. You can use your own, specific time-related problem. Follow the model and the illustrations shown to get a new, creative perspective.

Positive and negative consequences

Starting at 'Apply to self' and working round clockwise, the first pattern focuses on the problem-holder personally, rather than viewing the problem as a general one, or in an objective way. Often the problem reflects simply the person's own perceptions. They may feel themselves to be disorganised, even though friends and colleagues see them as examples of discipline and order. 'That's one way of looking at it' is another typical response that turns the problem into something personal. Probing the personal importance of the statement might also elicit values that are part of the problem. Asking 'Why is that important for you?' might move the problem towards the person's values and beliefs.

Just about everything has *some* positive consequence, so one or more possible outcomes can be suggested. You can be as creative as you like when thinking up responses. 'So you try harder?' or 'So there's no redundancy on the cards?' might change how you feel about the matter. Negative consequences are usually implicit in the problem statement, but others,

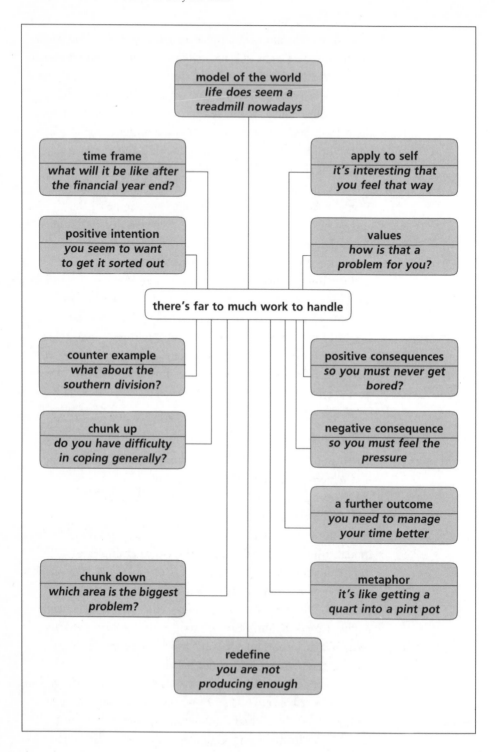

Fig. 19. Sleight of mouth.

perhaps more starkly negative, can stimulate thinking: 'So you'll give up?' or 'You'll have to find an easier job' or 'That's a recipe for a nervous breakdown'. Another outcome might be 'It's not the work that matters, but the way you worry about it.'

Redefine or suggest a metaphor

The metaphor or simile is not intended to provide a ready-made solution, but to set the creative right-brain working on associations that might give new perspectives, which in turn will give a better chance of a solution. All sorts of other simple analogies, whilst not directly relevant, might trigger the vital new thinking. 'It's like reaching the top of a mountain only to see another peak' is another example. The mountain analogy suggests there is always another challenge ahead. But each association with an analogy will reflect each person's individual background and experience, so will be unique. Redefinition can be as creative as you like. 'You can't manage your time' or 'You are not producing enough' are less radical responses, but might produce a change of thought pattern.

Chunking and counter-examples

Chunking down can go to any level. It might well be that the problem-owner has a jaundiced view of the situation simply because of a single task he is running late on. 'Which project is giving the problem?' might be a productive chunking-down reframe. Alternatively, the problem may relate to a conflict between work and home responsibilities, in which case a chunk down 'What is making it difficult for you to handle things lately?' might help. Similarly, chunking up can be to any level, and might also explore the home/work question in another way: 'Is the problem general throughout the company?', or 'Does this mean there is an upturn in business?' (The last response might also suggest a positive outcome, a redefinition. None of these patterns is a straightjacket, but rather a checklist to stimulate creativity.)

Counter-examples might include 'What about the southern division – they seem to cope'. Counter examples may start with, 'Yes, but ...'.

Positive intentions are similar to positive outcomes, but involve intention on the part of the problem-stater, and support the idea that behind every behaviour there is a positive intention. Possible intentions can be explored, such as 'You want to see a reorganisation?', or 'You want a bigger salary?' The time frame dimension might equally be explored: 'Has it got worse over a period?' or 'Will it get easier when you move nearer the office?' or even 'So will you be able to make the golf this weekend?' The 'model of the world' lifts the problem onto a cosmic level, or takes a 'helicopter' view.

Creativity checklist

Each of the 'angles' can have any number of comments or questions as responses, thus opening up scores – or hundreds if you like – of new perspectives on a problem. The chunking and metaphor patterns alone allow endless creative approaches.

This sort of technique is much more focused than traditional brainstorming methods. The patterns act as a mental checklist, avoiding creative blocks. Any time management problem, specific or general, can be subjected to the sleight of mouth technique. Don't worry if a particular pattern does not seem to apply, or you can't think of ideas. Just move round, and perhaps return to the pattern later.

This is a powerful technique you can use with specific problems. Try taking half a dozen time management problems or issues – work, social, domestic. You can be quite specific, if you wish:

'I can't seem to get round to clearing the garage', or
'I've been putting off doing so-and-so for months'

for example. The technique simply elicits different viewpoints, in feelings, and attitude as well as behaviour. It is like having a number of consultants rallying to your aid.

> All the creativity you need is within your own experience and brainpower.

The technique can be used in a group setting, in which case a wider range of responses might be generated. Otherwise it can be used on a DIY basis, as a checklist for creative perspectives.

Remember that one good idea can double your output and/or half the time you spend on a task or problem. Creative methods therefore offer a very high effort to result ratio. Because well-tried patterns are used as a checklist, even 'non-creative' people (if such existed) would find benefit in increased output and goal fulfilment.

Reversal

These reframing techniques are loosely termed *provocation techniques*. One version is known as 'reversal'. As the name implies a problem statement or 'truth' is reversed, to completely change its meaning. Issues or possibilities are then considered based on the new 'truth'. For example the problem: 'The monthly accounts are never out on time' might be reversed to 'The accounts are received punctually every month.' What might follow from the new 'truth'?

Questions or issues that arise are then 'brainstormed' for new ideas, assuming the reversal rather than the original statement is true. For example:

◆ What difference would punctual accounts make?
◆ What benefits, direct and indirect, might follow?
◆ Would they be used more widely and might they help in achieving budgets better?
◆ How punctual is punctual?
◆ What if they were 80 per cent accurate but issued five days earlier?
◆ What if they were 90 per cent accurate and circulated two days earlier?
◆ Who can input to this new target besides the accounts people?
◆ Could the accounts production be made cheaper as well as quicker?
◆ Who receives these punctual accounts?
◆ Who doesn't?
◆ Do they need all or only part of what is provided?
◆ Is any information not included which would be helpful?
◆ Why every month – what if they were completed weekly?
◆ Do our competitors have punctual accounts?
◆ Is punctuality more important than content?

◆ Is punctuality more important than accuracy?

Further lines of questioning will emerge as possible scenarios open up. The right-brain is involved in such techniques, as we may need to imagine a completely new situation, not as a written down abstraction but as a reality. You can mentally test out even the most ludicrous possibilities, and it is from these that real changes are likely to follow. This is a fairly typical work-based example, but you can apply the reversal process to *any problem you like.*

Do some pretending

Here is another example, which may be close to the heart of many non-numerate self-employed people: 'I hate doing VAT returns' (which probably means you spend twice as long as you need to on the job). Insert alternative words in place of 'VAT' and 'returns' – most of us hate doing something or other. The reversal would be: 'I love doing VAT returns', or something equivalent.

Visualising this new scenario, you might see yourself filling out the forms the day after you receive them, rather than at the last possible moment, having unnecessarily endured the nagging sense of guilt in the mean time. The chances are you will do your now 'enjoyable' task in peak energy time – maybe first thing in the morning, just as you would any favourite job, and so complete it more efficiently. As well as applying energy, just as to your favourite hobby, you will apply ingenuity and creativity to the task. Allow your creative mind to go to work:

◆ Can the job be made easier and even more enjoyable by changing how you do things?
◆ Is listing best done daily, weekly, or left to the end of the month?
◆ What about getting computer software for the job?
◆ Would that make the job more or less interesting?
◆ Would it save time?
◆ What about spin-off benefits?
◆ What about proving your numerary skills by halving the time you spend on the task?
◆ What about other jobs you enjoy? How do you start them?

How do you manage to get *them* finished on time?

◆ What is it about the job that you enjoy?

Use your imagination and be prepared to do some pretending. Imagine you are a person who fully believes the reversal to be true. We try to put ourselves in other people's shoes when truly empathising with a person we care for, so the skill is a natural one. The technique may seem absurd, but so are many of the best ideas when they first come to us. And so, also, may be the problem itself if it is based upon an irrational, negative self-belief.

Reframing self-beliefs

Reframing in this way is likely to bring some sense into what is probably an irrational situation. You may be labouring under a misplaced self-belief that you are 'no good with numbers', or a couple of negative memories involving VAT returns or VAT officials. You are free of course to carry on your hatred, and endure any consequences. But you are also free to change how you feel about any task, even if you stop short of actually enjoying it.

A more general belief 'I am hopeless at filling in forms' might be part of the real problem and can be changed using the same process.

> Nothing can remain the same perceptually after a serious attempt at reframing.

Although the initial reversal might seem ludicrous, it will at least offer the possibility of a radical, lateral rethink. The reversal itself can be carried out quite mechanically by a non-creative, left-brain thinker, so is an appealing and popular technique. The creativity, stimulated by the new 'truth', is then applied to any issues or opportunities the reversal suggests. This of course is the crucial part of the process, but can often be stimulated by reversals and rigorous self-questioning. Try applying the sleight of mouth model to the problem 'I am hopeless at filling in forms', or another personal one to which you have applied the reversal technique. This will show that there are different approaches to creativity, and you can choose the method that works best for you, or that seems to suit the actual problem.

Adding creativity

Techniques like this do not replace the need for creative thought. You will notice that in each case you have to exercise your own creativity, and the more creative you are, the better the insights and the more ingenious the solution. But the device does help to stimulate an otherwise lazy right-brain, and challenges some comfortable mind patterns. Use real problems. Reframing is not like a business game or simulation. It is a way to do what your mind can do quite well to start with – you just need to stimulate and harness it. It helps you to overcome the thinking habits that stop you seeing opportunities and having choices.

Making analytical tools creative

Even otherwise very powerful planning tools such as a SWOT (strengths, weaknesses, opportunities, threats) analysis can suffer from left-brain limitations. The four lists are usually rattled off quickly by seasoned managers attending a seminar, the same sort of exercise having been done, in different guises, in the past. By applying the reversal technique to each factor, completely new issues are raised and the tool becomes a highly creative one.

Your personal SWOT reversal

In terms of time management SWOT is a powerful personal self-management tool as well as a strategic business aid. Why not have a go at your personal reversed SWOT? First list each of your strengths, weaknesses, opportunities, and threats. If time is a major problem, some of the factors you list as weaknesses will reflect that. More likely, the list will reflect some of the real problems to do with not achieving goals. 'Procrastination', for example, might appear as a weakness. 'Good finisher' might be a strength. A forthcoming domestic upheaval that will eat up your time might be listed as a threat, and finishing your professional study course an opportunity to use your time on something completely different.

Then reverse each 'true' statement as the basis for a radical, lateral rethink. The issues emerging from such an exercise in self-awareness are likely to indicate where the big time saving can be made, and new ways to better achieve your outcomes.

Reframed force field analysis

Force field analysis is another popular problem-solving technique. It's a simple idea. Any outcome is subject to different 'forces'. Some help towards the outcome, while others hinder it, just like physical forces acting on an object from different directions. Once again, it can be used as a self-appraisal tool, as well as corporately.

Let's say a major client database review has been on the cards for ages, but somehow it has been postponed, and lately has created several fairly serious problems. Sooner or later the company is going to lose business. The force field (see Figure 20) identifies positive and negative forces acting on the outcome.

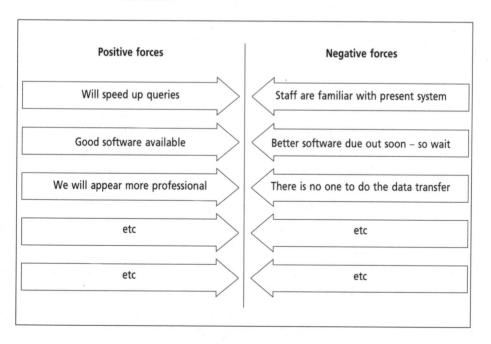

Positive forces	Negative forces
Will speed up queries	Staff are familiar with present system
Good software available	Better software due out soon – so wait
We will appear more professional	There is no one to do the data transfer
etc	etc
etc	etc

Fig. 20. Force field analysis. Outcome/task: Prepare client database.

This problem-solving tool is subject to the same weaknesses as the SWOT analysis. The obvious factors are identified, both positive and negative, such that any conclusion is likely to be no different from what you would have come up with ruminating on the problem yourself for a while. By reframing the factors further, however, a more creative solution might emerge. There will probably be factors you had not thought of at all.

We saw earlier the importance of how we feel and the way it affects our behaviour. Getting out on the wrong side of the bed, or whatever label we put on the feelings factor, might be the number one negative factor preventing us from achieving some outcome, yet might not even be on the list ('Don't feel like doing this job' [negative force]). Similarly, a basic dislike of doing lists, or organising systems, might be an overriding factor in our procrastination. Few people admit to these negative factors, and certainly will not incorporate the factor in a standard problem-solving technique ('Hopeless at organising information' [negative force]). So we come up with the same old solutions because we repeatedly fail to understand the real problem. The earlier negative and positive self-beliefs you identified in Chapter 4 will form additional – and perhaps vital – forces in any force field analysis.

Just as likely, we identify a factor but do not identify its importance and this misses the whole point of the force field analysis. One or two negative forces can counter a whole string of positive ones because of their negative *weighting*, and vice versa. We need insight – judgement, if you like – to realise the relative importance of the many factors at play. Applying the sleight of mouth technique, or reversal, can quickly suggest factors and their relative importance. Or a new problem emerges. Either way, you will be nearer to a solution.

A reframing mentality

Right-brain insights tend to come as 'aha' moments of surprise. Linear or analytical thought processes produce straightforward answers much like calculating the total when you add up a column of figures. Although you have control over the process, there are no big surprises. You move forward incrementally rather than by big jumps. An insight, however, can come at any time – maybe after incubating the problem. Moreover, the answer may not immediately fit the logic of the situation. As we saw earlier, this may mean you are 'in two minds'. But now you have a choice, a potentially better way. And choice is better than no choice.

I hope it will be obvious, that personal achievement, which is at the heart of time management, demands a special way of thinking. The danger is that techniques for releasing creativity can become as ineffective as the more analytically based tools, not least as they become familiar. There is no substitute for a reframing *mentality* – watching, listening, asking questions, and seeing things from a different perspective. Reversing any accepted truth, for instance, can become almost instinctive – a 'reversal mentality'. Super creativity exists all the time, just waiting to be released.

Outcomes and associations

There are two features about creativity that have to be allowed for. One is the outcome. Creativity does not happen in a vacuum – it addresses some need or outcome, such as 'getting away on holiday with a clear conscience'. The need may not be articulated and is below consciousness, although it will reflect the four basic needs we discussed in Chapter 5.

The second feature of creativity is associations. Each 'aha' moment seems to make some association – some link between disparate but otherwise insignificant factors. Both these factors are crucial to personal creativity and radical time management.

Creativity is a natural process, of course, and we will continue to get the odd blinding revelation or brilliant idea whether we have written down our goals or not, and whether we are ambitious or stick-in-the-mud by nature. That is because we all have outcomes – desires, needs – and we all have standard two-sided brains. But if our outcomes are not both conscious and clear, our lives will tend to be rather undirected. And that means poor use of time. Even 'inner peace', a fairly universal life goal (usually represented by other goals lower in our hierarchy), will not happen by accident. So the outcome emphasis is important.

Internally experiencing your outcome

In time management terms, the probing question might be: 'If I had two hours spare every day – or 20 a week, or whatever – what would I do with my time?' With well-defined, prioritised outcomes, the answer will not be difficult. But with such well-defined goals, the time problem is unlikely to arise in the first place, at least in the negative way it does for most time-pressured people. That is not all there is to it however. The truly effective goal, which draws on subconscious insights to help achieve it, is well *internalised*. That means that as well as being clearly defined in words (hence the importance of writing your goals down) you can experience it by way of internal representation systems – seeing, hearing and feeling. It becomes real where reality happens, on the landscape of the brain, rather than just in words or documents.

NLP has given us some further understanding and tools to apply this important principle far more effectively. Combining the goal clarification tests with mental rehearsing (sometimes called 'future pacing') *multiplies* your chances of achievement. You may also need to remove negative, or disempowering self-beliefs that are acting to stop you getting what you want, as described in Chapter 4.

These changes use the same basic skills of mental rehearsal or visualisation.

> We can reprogramme mental strategies that are not longer useful.

Being able to identify and manipulate your own thought submodalities is probably the biggest single way you can take control over your time and life. For most people, especially those who are left-brain-dominant, this requires some humility and plenty of practice, as does most habit-changing. Changes take place inside, rather than just on the outside. Such changes tend to be self-fulfilling – behaviour that 'fits' a belief further strengthens the new belief.

The power of association

Associations are just as central to creativity and change. The natural pattern-making tendency of the brain results in a well carved out mental landscape – mindsets that it is hard to break out of. This is essentially a survival system, offering amazingly fast recognition of concepts or things. It serves us best when things carry on much as they always did, in a linear, predictable way. When faced with an intractable problem, however, something is perceived to have gone wrong. We cannot immediately categorise the problem as one we have met and solved before, nor can we do so by breaking it down into its parts. The answer, in fact, lies somewhere else – it was just filed in the wrong place.

The idea of reframing is to make helpful associations outside our present thinking strategies, making the links that make sense, so helping us to achieve our goals. Insignificant facts take on special meaning when they are brought together and related to an outcome, a purpose.

Lifestyle and environment

Some people prefer to have lots of sensory stimuli going on around at the same time. For instance the TV or radio (or both) will be on while they are reading a book or newspaper. Rather than losing focus on what they are doing, they feel short-changed if they cannot mentally switch from one input to another at will. This is an acquired characteristic, of course, which train commuters seem able to perfect. These apparently wasted multiple sensory inputs can in fact provide a rich source of timesaving associations and goal-achieving insights.

Outcome and associations are central to time management for the simplest of reasons:

◆ They carry on working for you while you are using your time in whatever way you want to.

◆ You can literally do more than one thing at once – in fact a lot more than one thing.

The 'downtime' search for associations, for instance, can access billions of electro-chemical patterns in your brain – in short, your life experience. It then matches what it finds to a whole portfolio of current outcomes, both conscious and unconscious.

We simply cannot *consciously* process the billions of external stimuli from conversations, from what we read, and everyday sights, smells, tastes and sounds. But subconsciously those that 'fit' our outcomes are recorded and filed away for processing (maybe overnight) or result in the 'significance' of what we hear someone say, read, or see along the way. In other words, meaning is created. It is an inbuilt system for optimising your use of time.

We each have a unique, personal 'map' of reality, representing our self and the world we live in. For better or worse, this embraces all the values, beliefs and attitudes that dictate our behaviour. This results in our being where we are, what we are and who we are. Time – what it means to us, how we value it and what we do with it – is part of this map. Fortunately this is the 'software' of thinking, and can be reprogrammed.

> You can change how you feel, and remove the negative self-beliefs that are at the root of most so-called time problems.

Once we understand the importance of outcomes, our basic needs and desires, and the awesome effect of a change of attitude and belief, we can start to give direction to our lives – to take control. Using the simplest of intrinsic rewards you can motivate yourself to amazing feats. The key is self-knowledge, and the know-how to tap your creative mind. More than anything, you can start to draw on the more or less infinite resources of your creative right-brain. You can replace mediocrity with mastery – mastery over your time and what you do with it.

Books by the same author

NLP in 21 Days, (Piatkus)
NLP: The New Art and Science of Getting What You Want
Quick Fix Your Emotional Intelligence (How To Books)
Remembering Names and Faces (How To Books)
The Right Brain Manager, (Piatkus)
The Ultimate How To Book, (Gower)
Think Like a Leader, (Piatkus)

Index